The Arabian Cookbook

Thank you to the Al-Kafaât Catering School

Thanks for letting us borrow props, Mateus Stock, and Agneta Livijn.

The Arabian Cookbook

Traditional Arab Cuisine with a Modern Twist

RAMZI CHOUEIRY

Introduction by Bo Masser
Photos by Bruno Ehrs
Translation by Monika Romare

The original recipes in Arabic have been prepared directly by Chef Ramzi. The American versions of the recipes are somewhat revised according to American conditions and availability of ingredients. Therefore, they may vary slightly from the recipes that are written in Arabic.

الوصفات العربية اُعدّت مباشرة من قِبل الشيف رمزي.
الأنماط السويدية للوصفات معدّلة نوعاً ما لتلائم الظروف السويدية وإمكانية الحصول على المواد المكوّنة للوصفات.
ولهذا السبب فقد تكون مختلفة الى حدّ ما عن الوصفة الموجودة باللغة العربية.

Skyhorse Publishing

TABLE OF CONTENTS
المحتــويـــات

"Eating together and sharing different food cultures could perhaps build bridges between the people of the world."

Origin and Understanding

The Arab world has given its residents very special conditions for the production of food, by virtue of its geographical positioning. Long coastal environments, or large desert areas in the hinterland, are usually the two options people have in terms of environments to grow their food. Several historical high cultures have existed here, and many major trade routes passing through have contributed to Arab cuisine.

The region is a bridge between the Mediterranean and the Orient. My country, Lebanon, has been populated by people from all over the world ever since the Phoenicians. The country is a melting pot between different continents, and because of its rich nature and fresh water, many people have passed through or settled here. The Lebanese people have lived among many of the great civilizations within their borders: Greeks, Byzantines, Romans, Phoenicians, Turks, and the French. All of them have left a mark of their presence. And the Lebanese people have welcomed and respected all kinds of political and religious groups in their lush land.

Despite all of these powerful influences, the Lebanese kitchen has remained very traditional. On television, whenever I try to cook a fusion of Lebanese cuisine with other international cuisine, the reaction is always immediate. People do not like it! Viewers will call the studio and complain: "Make spaghetti or lasagna, but do not mix it with Lebanese food!" The viewers want to know all the secrets behind authentic Lebanese food.

However, my television audience also wants to learn about other food cultures. When you are aware of your own traditions and history, you may have an easier time understanding and respecting other cultures. Today, Arabic food, particularly Lebanese cuisine, has spread all over the world thanks to all the travelers that have stopped by. People meet up and enjoy a nice meal together. Eating together and sharing different food cultures could perhaps build bridges between the people of the world.

My dear father has taught me: "You own what you give—what you do not give, owns you."

I give to you my culinary heritage.

Chef Ramzi

The Smiling Chef

Anyone who has seen Chef Ramzi on satellite TV knows that he always smiles kindly. That is exactly how he greets us, all smiles, when we meet up with him for the collaboration on this cookbook. He gives a grand first impression, surely in scope, but mostly in charisma. Ramzi almost seems shy. He is careful whenever he reveals anything private about himself. For him, the road to the pots and pans has hardly been straightforward. However, in retrospect, each turn and step seems logical. Whenever Ramzi talks about the meaning of food, his encounters, or other cultures, he chirps and bubbles with joy and lowers his voice thoughtfully. Food is serious business for him. Food is joy. Meet Ramzi, the sunbeam from Beirut.

Ramzi Choueiry was born in Beirut in 1971 and has two sisters and a brother. The war in 1976 destroyed large parts of Beirut, including the Ramzi family's home. His father, Nadeem Shwayri, remained in the country while the rest of the family fled to Lyon, France. The nuns of *La Congrégation Notre Dame des Apôtres* had their headquarters there and actively helped Nadeem when he established the institute, *Al Kafaât*, in 1957, as they had already been good friends for a while.

Nadeem established a restaurant school as part of the *Al Kafaât* foundation. *Al Kafaât* means "ability" in Arabic, and the school was created to help young disabled people with financial difficulties.

Ramzi's mother, Lili, and the children stayed in France for a year and returned to Lebanon when the war was over in 1977. Ramzi's love for food and cooking was apparent early on in his life. Back in Lebanon, when he was six years old, he often used to help his mother stir food in the pots and pans. He still remembers the different aromas that would fill their kitchen.

Lili was forced to flee back to Europe with the kids three more times. During that time, Ramzi managed to complete a Bachelor of Arts degree in economics and law with good grades, and he was accepted to the University of Lyon II.

The son, and father Shwayri (the father prefers the English spelling), decided that the young Choueiry (Ramzi prefers the French spelling) should make the most out of his situation as a refugee. One summer, Ramzi applied to a branch of the University of London, in Bournemouth, to study the culinary arts.

Back in Lyon, he continued his second year studying economics and law. The lectures were usually held in the afternoons and evenings. Ramzi was eager to return to Beirut to support the *Al Kafaât* foundation. He saw it as an opportunity to learn more about the practical work in the restaurant business. The following year, he would get up at 4:30 AM to start work at 5:15 AM, and he would go on until noon, then take the bus back to the university. Above all, he was with Jean Masson at his world famous restaurant, *La Minaudière*.

When Ramzi returned to Lyon to complete his final year at the university, he had a new desire. He wanted to learn the secrets behind the French art of baking, and therefore, he apprenticed with master confectioner, Bernard Moine, president of the *Syndicat des Pâtissiers-Boulangers*. Eventually, Ramzi was appointed an honorary member of the association.

Ramzi Choueiry was now ready to return back home to Beirut. In 1993, he began reorganizing and modernizing the restaurant school based on what he had learned in Europe. The school curriculum was outdated, and he thought it would benefit from his new skills in the French art of baking and from the other European educational programs.

In February 1994, Ramzi was contacted by the newly founded Future TV, which was owned by Rafiq al-Hariri, the prime minister at the time. The first two years were recorded and broadcast only in Lebanon. Ramzi was soon regarded as a celebrity. In 1996, it was decided to broadcast the show on satellite TV. In the first episode, Ramzi cooked up a Lebanese menu and simultaneously answered phone calls from Dubai, Lebanon, Egypt, Iraq, and other parts of the world where his show now aired. Extra staff was added to the control room to cope with all of the incoming calls. After an hour had passed, the producer tiptoed in, waving his hands and gesturing: "Go on, go on!" The first episode ended up lasting for one hour and fifteen minutes. Today, the show airs daily hour-long episodes.

Future TV decided to publish a book with Ramzi's recipes featuring international cuisine that would appeal to the Arab market. Today, it has sold more than 600,000 copies. It is on its third edition, and nowadays he publishes and distributes the book himself. *Al Kafaât's* school of technology has launched a graphic design program and has invested in print presses from Heidelberg. The students publish a new edition of 5,000 copies every three months. All the profits from the publication are reinvested in the school.

The huge success of the book made it possible for Ramzi to realize a dream he had for a long time: a book about Lebanese cuisine and the country's cultural heritage. For two years he traveled around Lebanon and visited all the old cities and every single village in his beloved country. (Lebanon is about 124 miles long, and 31 miles wide, with about 4.2 million inhabitants.)

His second book, about Lebanese cooking written in Arabic, sold 20,000 copies in a few days. Today, the book has sold more than 150,000 copies. The first translation was in French. During the *Gourmand World Cookbook Awards* in 2003 in Barcelona, the French edition received the award for *Best Arabic Cookbook in the World*.

That same year, Ramzi's studio at Future TV in Beirut was hit by two bombs. The following day, Chef Ramzi chose to broadcast his cooking show live as usual, standing among the ruins and debris, despite the fact that one of the bombs had not been detonated. Many of his daily ten million viewers called in from around the world to express their sympathy and encouragement, condemning all acts of terrorism. After that, the cooking show was suspended for four months to rebuild the studio.

According to Ramzi, most Arabs like Lebanese cuisine. Arab cuisine is limited in general because of climate and geography. Most Arab countries consist of long coastlines with narrow, arable areas and large deserts in the hinterlands that affect food production. The selection of what can be grown is limited by nature. However, Lebanon has four clearly defined seasons, and it also has a rich source of water. These two factors make a huge difference compared to other Arab countries. Therefore, the Lebanese kitchen has a lot more options in terms of variety. All Arabs like it, as they recognize the flavors and keep the cuisine close to heart.

Meat has always been a luxury in Arabic cuisine, but today there are large farms with many cows and sheep. In Yemen, the famous spice market has existed for many centuries. Ships arrived here from India and to the Gulf region. The goods are transported through the Gulf via Lebanon, and then on to Europe. Thanks to this historic spice market, many dishes with rich sauces have been created from all the spices, usually together with another commodity—basmati rice. This used to be served mostly with fish. Food in the Gulf region is quite heavy, but not so varied. Dried fruit, butter, and spices are prevelant.

Saudi Arabia has its meat, *kabesh*, mixed with passed butter, *ghee*. The dish was developed to withstand the heat of the desert. With these limited conditions, only a few specialties can be found across the Arab world. Aside from Lebanon, only a few countries have a rich and varied food tradition. Morocco, Tunisia, Algeria, and Libya all have a very rich cuisine. There you can enjoy many wonderful dishes, especially recipes that are based on fish, meat, and poultry, but also a variety of sweets.

We are lucky to have been blessed with a milder climate, and we don't have any deserts, Ramzi explains. In Lebanon the range of fruit and vegetables is fantastic. We have coastal areas and the green Bekaa valley, with plenty of water, and a cool climate. Today we have many producers of meat, such as chicken, beef, and sheep. There is even some production of pork.

During the winter, all the mountain villages are covered in snow, and most of the roads are, or at least used to be, entirely blocked. The families became prisoners in their own homes. This led to the development of food processing in the summer and fall. Fruits such as apricots, grapes, and figs are sun dried on the roofs, and even vegetables like zucchini, eggplant, and tomatoes are preserved the same way. An important product for winter storage is *borghol*, a special type of wheat. It is added in *kibbeh* and *tabbouli*. *Borghol* differs from the bulgur that we usually get in the United States. It is thicker, more like whole grains.

A long time ago, before fridges and freezers existed, meat used to be preserved by different means. It was usually ground and cooked in fat, then stored in jars and covered with a white layer of fat. You could store meat for six months this way. The daily work used to be heavy during the winter, and it required heavy food. Today, it is difficult to find canned meat in grocery stores.

Due to its location, Lebanon was the first country in the region to build large hotels. It pioneered in tourism, which contributed to the development of the restaurant business and other professional ventures. Today, all hotels in the region request Lebanese chefs.

Lebanese chefs came up with different ways of using grapes. In the 1800s, when sugar was in short supply in the remote villages, they still wanted to create desserts. So they began using grape juice and simmered it over low heat until it thickened and had a concentrated sweetness. The syrup was used in baking cakes and biscuits, among other treats. The lemon tree is coastal and does not grow in the mountains. When the chefs couldn't get a hold of any lemons, they turned to grapes. They took the juice from unripe grapes, due to their high acidity, and used the juice in salads, such as *tabbouli*. Sweet and sour came from the same ingredient!

Lebanese cuisine has preserved many of the traditional ingredients by using several different kinds of vegetables, beans, grains, and olive oil. In many ways, it is healthy food. Raw onions and garlic are known to help maintain healthy blood pressure.

We were isolated during certain periods in the past decades, Ramzi says while lowering his voice. We lived in the country and were cut off from what was happening outside. All of a sudden, from 1992 to 1994, international chains such as McDonald's and Starbucks started appearing in Lebanon. It felt like there was a large opening to the world. People ran to the new spots to get a sense of something different from what they were used to. But they soon returned to what they liked the best. Today, Lebanese cuisine is still the number one choice in the region, and Lebanese restaurants attract more people than any others in the area.

In recent years a new phenomenon has occurred: the Lebanese cafe. This trend has become very popular, especially among young people. Lebanese cafes serve light snacks with Lebanese coffee and also offer hookahs. The hookah is popular among young people, but it is not at all a Lebanese tradition. The hotels often offer menus with a combination of Lebanese and European cuisine.

Ramzi takes me for a ride in his car, in the seemingly chaotic yet considerate traffic. "We have managed without law and order for decades, so we have learned to respect each other," he explains, alluding to the traffic that flows quite smoothly despite the large volume. It is his city, full of sentries and loud children. People wave to the TV chef and exchange a few words through the lowered car window. With one hand on the wheel, and one hand to the people, Ramzi radiates love and presence. Suddenly, we find ourselves behind a greengrocer who pulls his rickety wagon slowly ahead, and the traffic slows down. Ramzi breaks into a smile, bigger than ever, and turns to me:

"Seeing these men with their old-fashioned trolleys is like a memory from my childhood. But it also signifies a sense of high quality fresh fruits and vegetables. It is a symbol of hope: that the joy of food has a future in our modern and high-tech world!"

Bo Masser

Meze

Snacks & Dips

مقبـــلات مازة

Fatayer with Sleek
SMALL SPINACH PIES

12 PIECES

In the original recipe, sleek, greens that grow in the wilderness, are used. In the Unietd States we will have to settle for spinach, which is also commonly used in Lebanon today.

3 CUPS (375 G) FLOUR
2 CUPS (473 ML) OLIVE OIL
1 TEASPOON SALT
1 TEASPOON DRY YEAST
1⅓ CUPS (308 ML) WATER
2 CUPS (300 G) OF FINELY CHOPPED YELLOW ONION
3 TOMATOES, DICED
ABOUT 8 CUPS (250 G) FRESH SPINACH LEAVES
ALMOST 1 CUP (235 ML) LEMON JUICE

1. Mix flour and 1 cup of olive oil with salt and dry yeast. Heat water to 125°F (50°C), and add it to the mixture.

2. Work into a smooth dough. Cover with damp baking towel and allow to rise for 1 hour.

3. Heat the remaining 1 cup of olive oil in a large skillet. Fry the onion slightly without darkening it. Add the diced tomatoes.

4. Chop the spinach coarsely and add to the pan. Let it fry for a while.

5. Squeeze lemon juice over the mixture and remove the skillet from the heat.

6. Roll out the dough and cut out circles, about 3 inches (7.5 cm) in diameter.

7. Add a teaspoon of filling onto each circle, fold the sides together to form a triangle, and pinch the edges together.

8. Bake at 350°F (175°C), until the pies are golden brown. Serve them hot or cold.

فطائر بالسبانخ

عدد الحصص: ١٢ حبّة وسط تقريبًا

من النادر أن تعتبر بعض أصناف المعجنات كطبق أساسي، ووصفة الفطائر بالسبانخ هي من هذه النوادر. نستطيع تقديمها بحجم صغير أو كبير وهنالك مَن يستبدل حشوتها بالسلق والهندباء أو حتى بالخس العربي ولكن أطيبها ما كان بالسبانخ. في عميّق، قضاء البقاع الغربي، رأينا وصفة الفطائر ولكن بحشوة البقلة. وفي القرى البعيدة عموماً ليس استعمال السبانخ رائجاً كما هو عليه الحال في بيروت، ويمكن أن تكون البقلة هي أساس الحشوة ، أو ما توافر من سليق أي مختلف أنواع الحشائش البريّة المعروفة بالسليقة.

طحين ٣ أكواب
زيت ٣/٤ الكوب
ماء ١ كوب
خميرة ١ ملعقة صغيرة
سبانخ ٤ أكواب
بصل مفروم ناعم ٤ ملاعق كبيرة
صنوبر ٤ ملاعق كبيرة
سمَّاق ٢ ملعقة كبيرة
عصير حامض ١ كوب
زيت زيتون ١/٢ كوب

١- نصنع عجينة متماسكة من الطحين والزيت والماء والخميرة ورشة ملح.

٢- نترك العجينة ترتاح في مكان معتدل الحرارة ونضع عليها قطعة قماش مبللة كي لا يجفّ سطح العجين.

٣- في أثناء اختمار العجينة نقطع العروق من السبانخ ونغسله ثلاث مرات مع استعمال المطهّر في المرة الثانية. ثم يفرم ويعصر ويخلط مع البصل والصنوبر والسماق وعصير الحامض وزيت الزيتون، ويجب أن نحرص على أن تكون نكهة الحامض والسماق غالبة.

٤- ترق العجينة على الطاولة، وهنا يترك لكم تحديد درجة السماكة المرغوب بها، وتقطع أيضاً بحسب طلبكم، قطعاً كبيرة أو صغيرة وذلك باستعمال المقطع المناسب. ومن ثم نورّع الحشوة على الدوائر ونغلق الجهات الثلاث نحو الوسط بشكل نحصل معه على مثلّث، ومن ثمّ نخبزها.

Steeha from Baalbek

SMALL MEAT PIES FROM BAALBEK

25 PIECES

The secret behind the amazing taste is that the meat is cooked inside the dough. The original recipe calls for whole meat of lamb ribs, but in the United States it may be easier to find ground lamb.

Dough

ABOUT 1 CUP (225 G) BUTTER
ABOUT 8 CUPS (1 KG) OF FLOUR
1 TABLESPOON DRY YEAST
3 CUPS (710 ML) WATER

Filling

1 POUND (450 G) LAMB MEAT FROM THE RIBS, OR GROUND LAMB
1 POUND (450 G) TOMATOES
1½ YELLOW ONIONS
OPTIONAL: ½–1 RED CHILI AND ⅔ CUP (12 G) CHOPPED FLAT-LEAF PARSLEY, OR 2 TABLESPOONS TAHINI

1. Crumble the butter into the flour and add the dry yeast. Pour onto the work surface and make a hole in the middle. Heat water to 125°F (50°C), pour it into the pit, and work together to form a smooth dough.

2. Let the dough rise underneath a damp baking towel in a warm place, until it has doubled, about 1 hour.

3. Finely chop the meat if you are not using ground lamb. Mix with diced tomatoes and chopped onions. Add fine chopped chili and parsley, or tahini.

4. Squeeze the air out of dough and roll it out. Cut out circles in the dough, about 3 inches (7.5 cm) in diameter. Add a teaspoon of filling in the middle of each circle. Press the dough around the filling, and pinch the edges on four corners.

5. Bake at 350°F (175°C) for 10 to 15 minutes or until dough is golden brown. Serve hot or cold.

الصفيحة البعلبكيّة

الصفيحة عبارة عن عجينة بداخلها حشوة مرتكزة على اللحم. ويوضع اللحم بداخل العجينة وهو نيئ، غير مطبوخ. ويباشر بالاستواء داخل العجينة. ولربما كان هذا سرّ نكهتها الجيّدة.
وهناك طريقتان لتحضير الحشوة، وسنتكلّم عنهما.

العجينة:
طحين ٢ كيلو
سمنة ٢ كوب
ماء ٦ أكواب
خميرة ٢ ملعقة كبيرة

الحشوة رقم (١)
لحم غنم من الضلع ١ كيلو
بندورة ١ كيلو
بصل ٣

الحشوة رقم (٢)
لحم غنم من الضلع ١ كيلو
لبن ٥ أكواب
دبس الرّمان ١/٢ كوب

١- تحضّر العجينة وذلك بفرك الطحين مع السمنة ثم إضافة الخميرة إليه وإحداث حفرة في وسطه ووضع الماء فيها، ثم عجن المواد بعضها مع بعض حتى نحصل على عجينة متماسكة.

٢- نضع العجينة في مكان دافئ، بعيداً عن التيارات الهوائية، مغطاة بمنديل رطب حتى تختمر جيداً.

٣- ترق حينها وتُستخرج منها دوائر العجين باستعمالنا مقطع مستدير. ثم نحشوها بالحشوة التي نريد، ونطبق الجوانب على الحشوة بحيث تظلّ ظاهرة وتخبز بالفرن الحامي.

٤- أما الحشوة الأولى فتحضّر بفرم اللحمة يدوياً بالسيخ مع البندورة والبصل، مع إمكانية إضافة البقدونس أو الفليفلة الحرّة أو القليل من الطحينة.

٥- والحشوة الثانية تحضّر بفرم اللحمة يدوياً أيضاً بالسيخ، مع إضافة دبس الرّمان ثم اللبن، مع إمكانية إضافة البقدونس أو الفيفلة الحرّة أو القليل من الطحينة.

Manakish with Zaatar

LEBANESE PIZZA WITH ZAATAR

8 PIECES

Manakish is a relatively new phenomenon in Lebanon, but has quickly become a popular breakfast dish. A lot of it has to do with the fact that it is quick and easy to bake, plus it's cheap and tasty and can be varied endlessly with different fillings. It's shown here with zaatar, a popular spice mixture.

Dough

2 CUPS (473 ML) WATER
5 CUPS (625 G) FLOUR
1 TEASPOON SALT
1 TEASPOON SUGAR
1 TABLESPOON DRY YEAST
ALMOST 1 CUP (237 ML) OLIVE OIL, OR ANY OTHER VEGETABLE OIL

Zaatar

3 TABLESPOONS DRIED OREGANO
2 TABLESPOONS DRIED THYME
2½ TABLESPOONS SUMAC
1 TEASPOON SALT
⅓ CUP (29 G) ROASTED SESAME SEEDS
⅔ CUP (95 ML) OLIVE OIL

1. Heat water to 125°F (50°C). Mix flour, water, salt, sugar, and yeast. Add the oil. Work into a smooth dough.

2. Cover with a damp baking towel. Allow to rise for 30 minutes in a warm place.

3. Squeeze the air out of the dough and divide into eight small balls. Roll them out into circles, about 8 inches (20 cm) in diameter.

4. Mix the ingredients for the *zaatar* spice mix. Sprinkle it over the pizzas.

5. Bake at 475°F (250°C) for 7 to 10 minutes until the pizzas are golden brown. Serve at once.

المناقيش

عدد الحصص: ٢٤ حبّة صغيرة (قطرها ٨ سنتيمتر)
او ٨ حبّات كبيرة (قطرها ٢٠ سنتيمتر)

ظهرت المناقيش مؤخراً في لبنان، وتطورت حتى أصبحت اليوم الفطور الأكثر طلباً من قبل اللبنانيين. والسبب الأساسي هو سرعة وسهولة تحضيرها وانخفاض كلفتها، وطيبة مذاقها، وإمكانية تزاوجها مع مواد مختلفة لتعطي نكهات متعدّدة.

اشتهرت بعلبك بالصفيحة، وعنجر باللحم بالعجين، وجميع قرى الأقضية الجبلية بفطائر السليق، أو السبانخ، أو الخبز بالقاورما والبيض، أو بالكشك. وكانت كلّ ربّة بيت، عند عودتها من الحقل، تجهّز خلطة الزعتر وتورّعها على أرغفة الصاج.

صبّت كل هذه الأصناف اليوم تحت خانة واحدة هي المناقيش. واعتبر هذا آخر مثل لتطوّر المطبخ اللبناني التراثي القروي القديم، في التكيّف مع حاجيات ومتطلبات المستهلك الحديث، والتأقلم معها.

توسّعت دائرة إنتاج المناقيش إلى أن بدأنا نرى ظهور «مطاعم» مختصّة بتقديمها. فإذا بنا نرى اللبناني، يخرج إلى «مطعم»، ويتناول منقوشة ليلاً، ويعتبر ذلك عشاءً. والمنقوشة بالنهاية هي كناية عن عجينة تحضّر من طحين وخميرة وملح وسكر وزيت وماء، وبعد أن تعجن، يوزّع عليها أي من الحشوات المفضلة لدى الشخص. وقد تكلمنا عن ذلك بالتفصيل في قضاء البقاع الغربي، وبالتحديد في قرية عميّق. إليكم الآن وصفة العجينة التي أحضّرها دائماً:

طحين ٥ أكواب
خميرة ١ ملعقة كبيرة
ملح ١ ملعقة صغيرة
سكر ١ ملعقة صغيرة
زيت زيتون أو نباتي ١ كوب
ماء ٢ كوب

١- يخلط الطحين مع الماء والسكر والخميرة، ثم يفرك مع الزيت.

٢- نصنع حفرة بوسطه نضع فيها الماء، ونعجن المواد بعضها ببعض حتى نحصل على عجينة متماسكة.

٣- نغطي العجينة بمنديل رطب، ونتركها تختمر لمدة نصف ساعة.

٤- ترق بعد ذلك العجينة ونستخرج منها دوائر، ونوزّع عليها الحشوة التي نريد من:

– زعتر وسماق وسمسم مع زيت زيتون.

– جبنة عكاوي مبروشة.

– جبنة قشقوان مبروشة.

– كشك مع بصل مفروم ناعم ومكعبات بندورة.

– سبانخ مع صنوبر وبصل ناعم وسماق وزيت.

– حشوة اللحم بعجين.

– بيض بالقاورما.

Samboosik

MEAT-FILLED CRESCENTS

12 PIECES

Samboosik pies are a must on the Lebanese meze table. The name refers to the crescent shape. The original recipe calls for qawarma, which is mutton confit, replaced with ground lamb in this recipe.

3 CUPS (375 G) FLOUR
1 CUP (225 G) BUTTER
A PINCH OF SALT
1 CUP (237 ML) WATER
4 TABLESPOONS OLIVE OIL
18 OUNCES (500 G) GROUND LAMB
1 CUP (150 G) FINELY CHOPPED ONION
1 CUP (135 G) PINE NUTS
A PINCH OF SALT
A PINCH BLACK PEPPER
1 TEASPOON CINNAMON
1 TEASPOON GROUND CUMIN
1 CUP (245 G) GREEK YOGURT
VEGETABLE OIL FOR FRYING

1. Mix flour and butter until it has a crumbly texture.

2. Add salt and make a hole in the middle. Pour the water into the pit, and work into a dough.

3. Roll out dough and cut twelve circles, about 3 inches (7.5 cm) in diameter.

4. Heat the olive oil and fry the ground lamb, onions, and pine nuts until the mix gets a nice color. Season with salt, pepper, cinnamon, and cumin. Remove the skillet from the heat and stir in the yogurt.

5. Add a tablespoon of filling in the center of each circle. Pinch the edges together to form a crescent shape.

6. Fry in hot oil until they are nicely browned. Test if the temperature is right by dipping a piece of bread into the oil. If it comes out golden brown, the temperature is just right. Fry in batches, and allow the pies to drain on paper towels. Keep a lid nearby, in case the oil is set on fire.

السمبوسك

عدد الحصص: ١٢ حبّة وسط تقريبًا

من أهمّ المعجنات اللبنانية ومن ركائز المازه اللبنانية الحديثة. مثلما رأينا في مشغرة، نستطيع تقديم هذا الصنف مع حشوات حلوة وليس فقط مالحة. فالسمبوسك إذاً كناية عن عجينة وعن حشوة.

طحين أبيض ٣ أكواب
سمنة الكوب
ماء ١ كوب
ملح رشة
قاورما ٣ أكواب
بصل ناعم، صنوبر ١ كوب من كل صنف
لبنة ماعز ١ كوب

١– نفرك الطحين مع السمنة حتى نحصل على مزيج واحد أصفر اللون.

٢– نضيف الملح، ثم نحدث حفرة في الوسط ونضع فيها الماء ونعجن المواد حتى نحصل على عجينة متماسكة.

٣– لا نستعمل الخميرة أو البيض أو أية مادة أخرى رافعة لأننا سنقلي العجينة بالزيت وإذا كانت مختمرة سوف تفرقع ويتطاير الزيت الحامي في كل مكان.

٤– نرق العجينة على الطاولة، وبمساعدة مقطع مستدير نستخرج منها الدوائر.

٥– نضع القاورما على النار حتى تحمى وتسيل، عندها نضيف البصل الناعم والصنوبر ونحرّك حتى ينضج البصل، نطفئ النار ونضع اللبنة ونحرّك جيداً حتى تتوزّع المواد بعضها ببعض.

٦– كان باستطاعتنا أن نستعمل اللحمة المفرومة الخشنة بدلاً عن القاورما وعندما تنضج نطفئ ونضيف إليها البهار والملح والقرفة والكراوية لدعم النكهة.

٧– نوزّع الحشوة المحضرّة بداخل كل عجينة ونطبقها على بعضها ونلحمها بشكل جميل.

٨– نقلي حبات السمبوسك بالزيت العميق الحامي حتى تشقر، فترفع من الزيت وتقدّم.

ملاحظة: نستطيع أن نغيّر الحشوات، مثل استعمال حشوة الخضر عوضاً عن اللحم كالملفوف أو الفليفلة والجزر، أو بالجبنة أو بالجوز المجروش والمقلي بالزيت مع السمّاق، أو الحشوة الهندية أي الملفوف مع عروق الصوجا أو الصالصة الحرّة.

Kibbeh Mkabkabeh

HOLLOW GROUND LAMB CROQUETTES

25 PIECES

Kibbeh comes in all possible variations, and these happen to be hollow. The more skilled the chef, the prettier and larger the croquettes will turn out. The original recipe calls for goat meat, but we choose ground lamb.

ABOUT 3⅗ CUPS (500 G) BULGUR
2⅕ POUNDS (1 KG) GROUND LAMB
1 GRATED YELLOW ONION
SALT
BLACK PEPPER
3 TABLESPOONS FINELY CHOPPED YELLOW ONION
⅖ CUP (95 ML) OLIVE OIL
1 TABLESPOON OF "SEVEN SPICES"
OR:
    1 TEASPOON CINNAMON
    1 TEASPOON CUMIN
    1 TEASPOON CARAWAY, CRUSHED OR GROUND
    1 PINCH NUTMEG

1. Rinse the bulgur, and allow it to soak for 10 minutes. Drain, and mix with the minced meat and grated onion.

2. Salt, pepper, and knead the mixture thoroughly.

3. Mix the chopped onion with olive oil and the other spices for the filling.

4. Roll the ground meat mixture into balls, and make a hole in the middle of each ball with the index finger. Press lightly around the edges of the hole to make the hole larger.

5. Push a little bit of the filling into the opening, and close it up so that it forms a tip.

6. Grill, sauté, or fry the croquettes until they are golden brown.

كبة مكبكبة

نستعمل لهذه الوصفة المقادير المستعملة للكبة الزغرتاوية، غير أنّ المكبكبة لا تحتوي على حشوة الشحم.

والوصفة المكبكبة هي عبارة عن قرص كبة كبير الحجم، واسمها يدلّ على طريقة تحضيرها.

تؤخذ كمية من الكبة، تُفتل براحة اليد للحصول على الشكل الكروي، ثم تكبكب وتُعطى السماكة المطلوبة. وهنا تظهر مهارة الشخص في تحضير الأقراص التي قد يصل قطرها إلى الـ ١٠ سنتم.

أما كيفية التقريص أي صنع هذه الأقراص وكبكبتها فهي: بعد إعطاء الشكل الدائري للقطعة نبدأ بإدخال سبّابة الأصبع (مَلَى ٌ) في وسط كرة الكبة والضغط عليها نحو الخارج ونحن نلفها حتى يكبر حجمها وتفرغ من الداخل وتصبح على شكل كوب فارغ وبسماكة متساوية. نغلق الفجوة العليا إما بشكل خط مستقيم أو بطريقة جمع الفجوة لتأخذ الشكل المبوّز. تُخبز على الجمر.

ملاحظة: يمكن وضع حشوة اختيارية بحسب ذوق كل شخص، فقد تكون قلية بصل ولحم مفروم ناعم، أو قاورما، أو غيرها بحسب الذوق. كما يُمكننا أيضاً أن نقلي هذه الكبة في زيت عميق بدلاً من شيّها على الفحم.

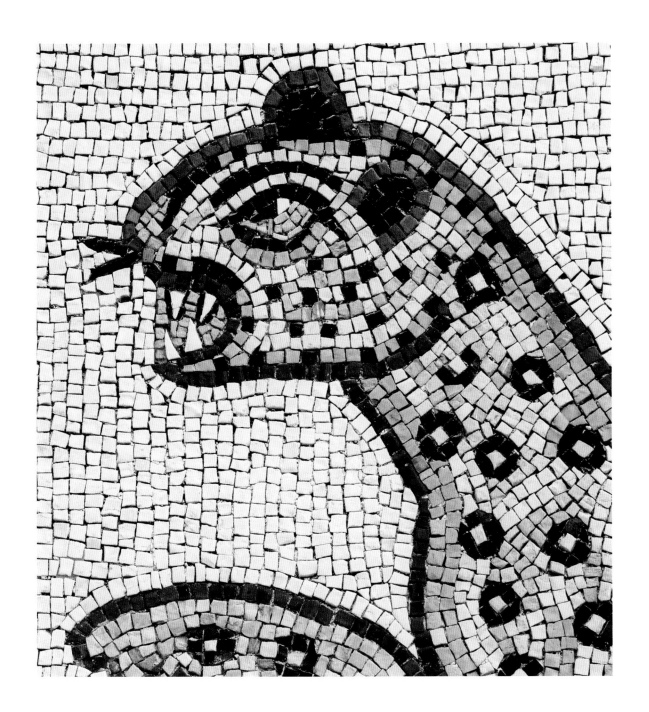

Baba Ganoush

LEBANESE EGGPLANT DIP

SERVES 4

One of the key elements on the meze table. Eggplants are common in the Lebanese kitchen and occur in many dishes.

2 LARGE EGGPLANTS
⅔ CUP (100 G) TAHINI
⅔ CUP (95 ML) LEMON JUICE
2 TEASPOONS MINCED GARLIC
SALT
OLIVE OIL

1. Wash the eggplants and pierce them with a sharp knife to prevent them from cracking in the oven.

2. Place them in an ovenproof dish and roast them at 475°F (250°C) for 15 to 20 minutes. You can also sauté them on the stove.

3. Take them out when they have turned completely black, and peel them under running water. Drain in the colander for 15 minutes.

4. Chop them coarsely and run them in the blender with tahini, lemon juice, garlic, and salt.

5. Pour into a small bowl and make a hole in the middle. Fill the hole with olive oil and garnish with pomegranate seeds or diced tomatoes.

بابا غنّوج

عدد الحصص: ٤ إذا قدّمت كمقبلات

يتنافس البابا غنوج أو المتبّل مع الحمّص على احتلال المرتبة الأولى في المازه اللبنانية. يُحضَّر في الغرب بطريقة متشابهة، ولكن مع غياب الطحينة، ويُسمّى «كافيار الباذنجان». ويلعب الباذنجان دوراً مهمّاً في الطبخ اللبناني ونجده بوصفات عدّة. ولكن وصفتنا هذه هي الوحيدة التي تستعمل لبّ الباذنجان، مما يعطيها النكهة اللذيذة. وكما مع الحمّص، فإنّ عصير الحامض الطبيعي، والثوم المدقوق، يحدثان توازناً مع الطحينة، فتتعادل النكهات، ونصل إلى هذا الصنف اللبناني من المقبلات الباردة في المازه.

إليكم الآن طريقة تحضيره.

باذنجان ٢ حبة كبيرة
طحينة ١/٢ كوب
عصير حامض ١/٢ كوب
ثوم مدقوق ٢ ملعقة صغيرة
ملح حسب الرغبة

١- يُغسل الباذنجان جيدا، ثم نحدث ثقوباً في قشرته برأس السكين لئلاّ تنفجر الحبة في الفرن.

٢- نضع الباذنجان في صينية، وندخله الفرن حتى ينضج، أو نشويه على النار.

٣- يقشّر الباذنجان تحت الماء البارد، ويُحفظ اللبّ في مصفاة لمدّة ربع ساعة.

٤- يُفرم اللب فرماً خشنا، ويُضرب على آلة الفرم مع الطحينة، وعصير الحامض، والثوم، والملح.

٥- يُزيّن وسط الصحن بالرّمان، أو مربعات البندورة الحمراء، وزيت الزيتون.

Hummus

CHICKPEA DIP WITH SESAME PASTE

8 SERVINGS

Hummus means "chickpeas" in Arabic. It is also one of our most important appetizers, but it can also be served with grilled meat.
Preferably, we make it with dried chickpeas that have been soaked overnight, but you can also use canned chickpeas.

4 CUPS (ABOUT 800 G) DRIED CHICKPEAS
2 TEASPOONS BAKING SODA
WATER
⅔ CUP (100 G) TAHINI
2 TEASPOONS MINCED GARLIC
⅔ CUP (95 ML) LEMON JUICE
SALT
OLIVE OIL

1. Clean and rinse the chickpeas and let them soak in water together with a teaspoon of baking soda overnight.

2. Rinse and drain. Place them in a saucepan, cover with cold water, and add a teaspoon of baking soda. Boil over high heat until the chickpeas have softened, about 1 hour.

3. When the chickpeas are done, the shells will float to the surface. The more peels you remove, the better the result.

4. Mix the chickpeas into a paste while they are still warm.

5. Add tahini, garlic, lemon juice, and salt. The flavor can be varied according to quantities of each ingredient. Decorate with whole chickpeas and olive oil before serving.

الحمّص بالطحينة

عدد الحصص: ٤ إذا قدّمت كمقبلات

عندما كنتُ أتجوّل فوق قمة جبل الأربعين وأتمتّع بالمناظر الواسعة الخلابة، وكذلك في قضاء سير الضنيّة - طرابلس، الذي يمتدّ أمامنا حتى يصل إلى شاطئ البحر، إذا بي أمرّ بالقرب من حقل حمّص، فتوقفت. ما أطيب الحمّص الأخضر! حينئذ تذكّرت قرية قوسايا في قضاء زحلة حيث أخبرني الأهالي كيف كانوا في الماضي وفي سهرات الصيف يتجمّعون حول «الأبولة» ويشوون الحمّص الأخضر. وقد تطوّر استعمال الحمّص، طبعا، وأصبح عنصراً أساسياً في المونة اللبنانية، ولاسيّما بعد أن يُجفف. يُنقع قبل ليلة بالماء، ثم يُسلق، وبعدها يُطحن، ويُطيّب بالثوم والطحينة وعصير الحامض، ويُزيّن بزيت الزيتون. وقد تجاوز الحدود اللبنانية فوصل إلى أوروبا وأميركا حيث نجده على رفوف أهم متاجر الأكل.

إليكم الآن طريقة تحضيره:
حمّص ٤ أكواب
عصير الحامض ١/٢ كوب
طحينة ١/٢ كوب
ثوم مدقوق ٢ ملعقة صغيرة
ملح حسب الرغبة

١- يُنقى حب الحمص ثم يُغسل ويُنقع بالماء البارد طيلة الليل.

٢- في اليوم التالي، يُغسل الحمّص مجدداً ويوضع في طنجرة، ويُغمر بالماء البارد ويوضع على نار قوية حتى ينضج. نستطيع أن نضيف إليه في هذه المرحلة نصف كمية البيكاربونات المتبقية إذا كنا قد وضعنا النصف الأوّل في ماء النقع (يوضع ٣٠ غرام بيكاربونات لكيلو الحمّص).

٣- استعمال البيكاربونات هو اختياري. فهنالك مَن يُكثر من استعماله، وهناك مَن لا يُدخله إلى مطبخه، لكونه مُعطّلاً للفيتامينات الموجودة في المواد.

٤- عندما ينضج الحمّص، نلاحظ ظهور قشر الحب على سطح الماء. يستحسن إزالة قدر كبير من القشر الذي يؤثّر على النكهة النهائية.

٥- تطحن الحبوب حتى تنعم، ويستحسن فعل ذلك عندما يكون الحبّ ساخنا.

٦- تضاف الطحينة وتحرّك جيدا، ثم الثوم وعصير الحامض والملح. ويمكننا أنْ نعدّل النكهة حسب رغبتنا بإضافة أيّ من المواد المذكورة. ونستعمل أحياناً القليل من الماء المبرّد بالثلج لإعطاء الحمّص اللون الأبيض.

ملاحظة يبقى الحمّص من أهم مقبلاتنا، ويرافق المشاوي المختلفة. ونستطيع تقديمه أيضاً مع قاورما اللحمة أو شاورما اللحمة التي نضعها في وسطه.

Tabbouli

PARSLEY SALAD WITH BULGUR

4 SERVINGS

A popular salad that can be served with anything. At my cooking school, we are proud to have made the world's largest Tabbouli at 7,841.8 pounds (3,557 kg), which got into the Guinness Book of Records.

3 TOMATOES
2 YELLOW ONIONS
4 CUPS (125 G) CHOPPED PARSLEY LEAVES
⅖ CUP (12 G) CHOPPED FRESH MINT
¾ CUP (105 G) BULGUR
1½ TEASPOONS SALT
¾ TEASPOON BLACK PEPPER
⅖ CUP (95 ML) LEMON JUICE
⅖ CUP (95 ML) OLIVE OIL

1. Wash the tomatoes, slice them thinly, and cut them into small pieces.

2. Finely chop the onion. Mix it in a bowl together with the tomatoes, chopped parsley, and mint.

3. Rinse bulgur twice, press out all the water, and add the vegetables, salt, pepper, lemon juice, and oil. Mix thoroughly.

4. Serve cold. Decorate with lettuce leaves and lemon wedges.

التبّولة

عدد الحصص: ٤

بقدونس ٣ باقات
بندورة حمراء ٣ حبات متوسطة
بصل ٢ حبة متوسطة
نعناع ١/٢ باقة
برغل ناعم ٣/٤ الكوب
عصير حامض ١/٢ كوب
زيت زيتون ١/٢ كوب
ملح ١ ١/٢ ملعقة صغيرة
بهار ٣/٤ ملعقة صغيرة

١- تُنقى باقات البقدونس والنعناع من الأعشاب الدخيلة والأوراق الصفراء، ثم تغسل جيداً، وتترك لتجف من ماء الغسل، بعدها تفرم فرماً ناعماً مع الحرص على عدم وجود عروق أو أوراق صفراء.

٢- تغسل البندورة وتنزع منها العين الخضراء ثم يُصار إلى تقطيعها إلى شرحات رفيعة بالطول ومن ثم إلى مكعبات صغيرة الحجم.

٣- يفرم البصل فرماً صغيرا، ثم تخلط المواد التي تمّ تحضيرها في وعاء.

٤- يغسل البرغل الناعم مرتين ثم يُصفَّى جيداً ويوضع على المواد المحضّرة مع البهار والملح والحامض والزيت وتقلب جميع المواد.

٥- يجب أن يُحافظ البرغل على القليل من قساوته، لذلك يُغسل ويُضاف مباشرة قبل التقديم.

Fattoush
TART SALAD WITH TOASTED BREAD

2–3 SERVINGS

This refreshing salad is an important dish during Ramadan, because its fresh and healthy ingredients complement the dishes that are served during the fasting month.

2 SMALL CUCUMBERS
3 TOMATOES
5 RADISHES, SLICED
OPTIONAL: ⅖ CUP (12 G) PURSLANE
⅖ CUP (12 G) MINT LEAVES
⅖ CUP (12 G) FRESH SAVORY
1 SMALL YELLOW ONION
3 SCALLIONS
1 ROASTED OR FRIED LIBA OR PITA BREAD
⅖ CUP (95 ML) OLIVE OIL
1½ TEASPOONS MINCED GARLIC
⅕ CUP (47 ML) LEMON JUICE
2 TABLESPOONS SUMAC

1. Cut the cucumber and tomatoes into equal-sized cubes. Add the radish slices, but save some for garnish.

2. Mix purslane (if you have it), mint, and savory with the chopped vegetables, sliced yellow onion, and shredded scallions.

3. Break the bread into pieces and mix half of it with the vegetables. Make a dressing with olive oil, garlic, lemon juice, and half of the sumac. Drizzle over the salad.

4. Garnish with the remaining bread pieces, sumac, and radish slices.

الفتوش

في شهر رمضان الكريم، يلعب الفتوش دوراً مهماً، فهو الصنف المُنعش في لائحة الطعام. الفتوش مزيج من تشكيلة واسعة من الخضار الطازجة، يُرافقها الخبز المحمّص أو المقلي وصلصة رائعة مؤلفة من زيت الزيتون والثوم وعصير الحامض والكلّ مطيّب بالسمّاق.

خيار وبندورة ٣ حبات من كل صنف
فجل مقطع دوائر ٥ حبات
نعناع، بقلة، زعتر ١/٢ باقة من كل صنف
بصل يابس ١ حبة
بصل أخضر ٣ عروق
خبز محمّص ١/٤ رغيف
زيت زيتون ١/٢ كوب
ثوم ١ ١/٢ ملعقة صغيرة
عصير حامض ١/٤ كوب
سمّاق ٢ ملعقة كبيرة

١- يقطع الخيار والبندورة إلى مكعبات صغيرة متشابهة ويُضاف إليها الفجل، ولا يُقشر الخيار والفجل وذلك للاحتفاظ بلونها.

٢- تنقّى أوراق البقلة والزعتر والنعناع وتغسل جيداً وتصفّى من الماء وتُضاف إلى باقي المواد كما يُفرم البصل اليابس بشكل جوانح والبصل الأخضر إلى قطع صغيرة حيث تضاف أيضاً إلى المواد الأخرى.

٣- يُكسر الخبز المحمّص إلى قطع صغيرة ويوضع قسم منها مع بقية المواد وتُخلط جيداً مع الحامض والزيت والملح وقسم من السمّاق.

٤- يُزيّن سطح الفتوش بباقي الخبز المحمّص والفجل المقطع وما تبقّى من السمّاق.

Yabrak with Meat

STUFFED GRAPE LEAVES

6 SERVINGS

Many Lebanese dishes consist of stuffed vegetables. Sometimes there is meat in the filling, and at other times the filling is vegetarian. We have replaced whole lamb with ground lamb. The same filling is used for stuffed zucchini. In the photo, you see ghammeh, a type of sausage that is filled with a similar rice blend.

ABOUT 1⅓ CUPS (225 G) SHORT-GRAIN RICE
ABOUT 1½ POUNDS (650 G) GROUND LAMB
OPTIONAL: TWO TOMATOES
ABOUT 2 POUNDS (900 G) GRAPE LEAVES (OR SMALL ZUCCHINI)
POTATOES
BEEF BROTH
LEMON JUICE

1. Mix the rice with ground lamb. You can also add some chopped tomatoes.

2. Put some filling in the center of each leaf (or inside the hollowed-out, small zucchini) and roll into a finger-thick dolma.

3. Place the dolmas (or zucchini) in a pot whose bottom is covered with potato slices. Pour broth over the dolmas until they are covered, and squeeze some fresh lemon juice on top. Place a weight on top so that the dolmas don't open up, and boil over medium heat until the rice is cooked.

يبرق باللحمة

من أهمّ الأطباق في لبنان أصناف الخضار المحشوة بحشوات الأرز باللحم، أو باللحم وحده، أو بالأرز والخضار.

ومن أشهر هذه الوصفات ورق العنب المحشو باللحمة والأرز، أو بالخضار والأرز. وهذه الأخيرة وصفة قاطعة صيامية سنتكلّم عنها في قضاء زغرتا.

أما الوصفة باللحمة فقد رأيتها في عدّة أقضية تحضّر بشكل طبيعي في المنازل التي زرتها.

ورق عريش ١ كيلو
لحمة ضلع مفرومة ناعمة ٧٥٠غرام
أرز مصري ٢٥٠ غرام

١- تحضّر حشوة اللحم بخلط الأرز المصري مع اللحم المفروم الناعم، والقليل من البندورة المقطّعة، إلى مكعبات صغيرة وبالنسب التي نريدها. والبندورة اختيارية.

٢- نضع القليل من الحشوة في وسط كل ورقة، ونطبقها على الحشوة، ونلفها بعضها إلى بعض بحيث نحصل على أصابع صغيرة.

٣- من الممكن صفّ الأوراق في وعاء كعبه مغطّى بشرحات البطاطا، وغمرها بمرقة عظام الغنم مع القليل من عصير الحامض، وطبخها على نار متوسطة حتى النضوج الكامل. أو من الممكن استعمال الكوسى المحشو معها والكستليته التي تلعب دورا مهماً بإعطاء النكهة القوية الدسمة.

٤- في جميع الأحوال، يفترض وضع صحن على سطح الأوراق وعليه وعاء أصغر بداخله ماء، وذلك لخلق ثقل على الأوراق كي لا تتفتّح خلال الطبخ.

٥- يقدّم اليبرق مع الكستليته والكوسى والفوارغ والكروش والكراعين، أي المقادم، ويعتبر من أهم الأطباق اللبنانية.

Maqaneq

LEBANESE LAMB SAUSAGE

35 PIECES

Maqaneq is a type of sausage that is common on the hot meze table.
The taste varies according to the butcher who has prepared them. However,
if you feel ambitious, you can make them from scratch.

18 OUNCES (500 G) LEAN BEEF
18 OUNCES (500 G) LAMB BRISKET
18 OUNCES (500 G) LAMB FAT
1 TABLESPOON CINNAMON
1 TABLESPOON PAPRIKA
1 TABLESPOON GROUND GINGER
2 TEASPOONS GROUND CLOVES
1 TEASPOON GROUND NUTMEG
2 TEASPOONS MAHLAB (OPTIONAL)
1 TABLESPOON CAYENNE PEPPER
CHOPPED FRESH CORIANDER ACCORDING TO TASTE
PINE NUTS ACCORDING TO TASTE
ANY WHITE OR RED WINE, OR BRANDY
3 LAMB SAUSAGE CASINGS

1. Finely grind the beef, lamb meat, and the lamb fat together.

2. Season with the ground spices and the fresh coriander. Add
   the pine nuts, and mix well. If you want to, you can add a
   little bit of wine or brandy.

3. Thread the casing onto a sausage stuffing horn, and fill with
   the sausage batter until the casing is full.

4. Turn the filled sausages at regular intervals so that the sausages become as long as desired.

5. Let the sausages hang and dry overnight. They taste even
   better if you sauté or grill them the following day.

المقانق

عدد الحصص: ٣٠ حبّة تقريبًا

تنتمي وصفة المقانق إلى المازة اللبنانية الساخنة وهي وصفة مرتكزة كاملاً على اللحام،
فهو الذي يحضرها ومن خلالها تظهر مهارته وذوقه.
هي كناية عن لحم تمّ فرمه ناعماً ثم طيّب وأعطي الشكل النهائي بمساعدة مصران
الغنم الذي يقلب بالهندسات.
نستطيع بعد ذلك قليه أو شويه.

لحمة بقر ١ كيلو
زور غنم٥٠٠ غرام
ليّة ٥٠٠ غرام
قرفة ١٠ غرام
بهار حلو ١٠ غرام
زنجبيل ١٠ غرام
قرنفل ٥ غرام
جوزة الطيب١٠ غرام
محلب ٥ غرام
حرّ١٠ غرام
كزبراء يابسة حسب الرغبة
مصران غنم ٣
صنوبر حسب الرغبة

١- نستعمل كميات متعادلة من الهبرة (لعبة بقر) ومن الدهن (زور وليّة) فذلك يعطي
نكهة أطيب بالنهاية

٢- نباشر بفرم الهبرة والدهن معاً فرماً ناعماً.

٣- نضيف عليها البهارات والكزبراء اليابسة والصنوبر وتخلط المواد مع بعضها
البعض مع إمكانية إضافة القليل من النبيذ الأحمر والأبيض والكونياك وذلك بشكل
اختياري.

٤- بعدما تمّ تجهيز الحشوة نباشر بتوزيعها بداخل المصران وذلك بمساعدة قمع
مخصص لذلك.

٥- عندما يمتلئ المصران بالحشوة نباشر باعطاء الشكل النهائي وذلك بتمريهم بين
بعضهم والحصول على القطع.

٦- يعلّق المصران أو المقانق حتى تصفي جيداً وتربح النكهة إذا تركت لليوم الثاني.

Octopus in Ink

6–8 PORTIONS

This dish is available in different variations in several parts of the world. It has been popular in Lebanon for a long time and is a common feature on the meze table, when it consists of fish and shellfish.

2⅕ POUNDS (1 KG) LARGE OCTOPUS
⅔ CUP (95 ML) VEGETABLE OIL
1½ CUPS (225 G) CHOPPED YELLOW ONION
1½ CUPS (ABOUT 250 G) SLICED CARROTS
1 CUP (150 G) SHREDDED LEEKS
SALT
WHITE PEPPER

1. Clean the octopus by gripping the head and grabbing the intestines as far in as possible. Then pull them out. If the hard transparent part does not come out, remove it separately. Save the ink bladder. Rinse the rest of the squid with cold water and dry with paper towels.

2. Cut the octopus into pieces.

3. Heat the oil in a saucepan and add the onion.

4. Add the octopus pieces after a few minutes and stir.

5. Mix all the ingredients together, then add the ink diluted with water so that the remaining ingredients are covered.

6. Bring to a boil, cover with a lid, and allow to simmer for half an hour over medium heat. Stir occasionally to avoid burning.

7. Take out the squid pieces and place them on a serving platter. Strain the sauce over them, and serve.

صبيدج (أخطبوط) بحبره

عدد الحصص: ٦-٨

تنتمي هذه الوصفة إلى المطبخ العالمي إذ نجدها بعدّة مطابخ. ولكن في لبنان لاقت نجاحاً كبيراً منذ السنين البعيدة، وأصبحت من أهم وصفاتنا البحرية، لا بل تعتبر من أهم أصناف المازه البحرية. وهنالك عدّة طرق لتحضيره ولكن الأفضل هي مع حبره.

وقبل البدء بطبخه، يجدر بنا أن ننظفه باستخراج العظمة الموجودة في ظهره، ونزع كيس الرمل والحبر، فنحتفظ بكيس الحبر ونرمي الباقي. كما يوجد أيضاً كريات بيضاء صغيرة في رأسه يستحسن نزعها ورميها وذلك لعدم استفادتنا منها من حيث النكهة، خاصة وأنها أحياناً تكون قاسية مزعجة عند الاستهلاك.

يغسل بالماء الباردة فيصبح جاهزاً للطهي.

صبيدج ١ كيلو
بصل مقطع جوانح ١ ١/٢ كوب
جزر ١ ١/٢ كوب
كراث مقطع ١ كوب
زيت نباتي ١/٢ كوب
ملح وبهار أبيض حسب الرغبة

١- نقطع الصبيدج إلى قطع متوسطة الحجم.

٢- نضع الزيت في وعاء على النار، وأول ما يحمى نضيف عليه البصل.

٣- بعد بضع دقائق، نضيف قطع الصبيدج، ونباشر بالتحريك حتى تقلب المواد جيدا.

٤- نضيف عندها الكراث والجزر والملح والبهار.

٥- تقلب المواد بعضها ببعض جيدا، ونضع غطاء على الوعاء، ونتركها لمدة نصف الساعة على نار متوسطة، أو في الفرن مع التحريك بين الحين والآخر كي لا تلتصق المواد في كعب الوعاء.

٦- نذوب بعدها كيس الحبر بالماء الكافي لغمر المواد في الوعاء، ونترك الوصفة على نار قوية حتى تغلي، ومن ثم على نار متوسطة حتى تصل إلى النضوج التام.

٧- نستخرج عندها قطع الصبيدج من الصالصة، ونضعها في جاط التقديم، ونصفّي عليها الصلصة السوداء.

Pita Pizza

SERVES 4

This is a very easy version of pizza, and it is often served with anything grilled. It is usually folded and eaten with hands.

⅖ CUP (100 G) TOMATO PUREE
2 LARGE LIBA OR PITA BREADS
1 RED ONION
⅕ CUP (24 G) CHOPPED FLAT-LEAF PARSLEY
2 TEASPOONS SUMAC
SALT

1. Spread tomato puree over the breads.

2. Peel and slice the red onion. Mix with parsley, sumac, and salt, and sprinkle the mixture over the bread.

3. Cut into pizza slices.

4. Serve as an accompaniment with anything grilled. You can also bake the pizzas briefly in the oven.

خبز للمشاوي

أربع حصص

نوع من البيتزا السهلة التحضير تُقدم غالباً مع وجبات اللحم المشوي. يتم طويها وتناولها باليد لأكلها.

١ ديسيلتر معجون الطماطم
٢ رغيف خبز عربي
١ بصلة حمراء
٢ ديسيلتر بقدونس مفروم
٢ ملعقة شاي سماق

ملح

١– أنشر معجون الطماطم على الخبز.

٢– قشّر وأقطع البصلة الحمراء الى شرائح. أخلطها مع البقدونس والسماق والملح وأنشر الخليط على الخبز.

٣– قطّع الخبز الى قطع.

٤– تُقدم كملحق أضافي للوجبات المشوية. يمكن أيضاً وضع قطع البيتزا في الفرن لفترة قصيرة.

Mousakhkhan

CHICKEN WRAPS FROM PALESTINE

SERVES 4

Mousakhkhan is a popular dish in Palestine, where it is served in various shapes. Here, the sumac-flavored chicken has been rolled in flat bread.

1 CHICKEN (1 LB/450 G)
2 BAY LEAVES
1 CINNAMON STICK
1 LEEK
5 TABLESPOONS OLIVE OIL
2 CUPS (300 G) THINLY SLICED YELLOW ONION
3 TABLESPOONS SUMAC
2 MARKOUK BREADS, LIBA BREAD, OR ANY OTHER TYPE OF FLAT BREAD

1. Place the chicken in a large pot and cover it with water. Add the bay leaves, cinnamon stick, and leek (that has been cut into pieces). Boil for about 1 hour, or until the chicken is cooked. Skim off the skin. Chop chicken.

2. Remove the bones from the chicken and place the meat aside for now.

3. Heat 2 tablespoons of oil in a saucepan and add the onion. Allow it to get some color, then add the sumac. Stir well so that the onions will taste like sumac.

4. Cut the bread into ten triangles. Cut the chicken into small pieces and spread some chicken pieces and the onion mixture over each triangle, and roll them up. Place the rolls on the bottom of an ovenproof dish and brush with the remaining oil.

5. Place the dish in the oven at 400°F (200°C) for 15 to 20 minutes or until the bread is crispy.

6. Eat with your hands.

مسخّن

دجاجة واحدة (١٤٥٠ غرام)
ورق غار ٢ ورقة
عيدان قرفة ١ عود
بصل مفروماً فرماً ناعماً ٢ كوب
كراث ١ عرق
سمّاق ١ كوب
زيت نباتي ٥ ملاعق كبيرة
خبز مرقوق ٢ رغيف

١- نسلق الدجاج مع المواد المعطّرة، أي ورق الغار والقرفة والكراث، بعد تنظيف سطح الماء من الأوساخ التي تظهر.

٢- عندما ينضج الدجاج نفصل لحمه عن عظمه وجلده ونضعه جانباً.

٣- في هذه الأثناء، نضع ملعقتين كبيرتين من الزيت في طنجرة على النار، وعندما يحمى نضيف إليه البصل المفروم فرماً ناعماً.

٤- نحرّك البصل ونتركه حتى يتغير لونه، ونضيف إليه السمّاق ونحرّك جيداً حتى يمتصّ السمّاق كل الزيت ويستوعب البصل جيداً .

٥- نقطع رغيف الخبز المرقوق الى ١٠ مثلثات ونضع عند رأس كل مثلث القليل من الدجاج والسماق والبصل ونلفه بشكل السندويش الصغير، ونضعه في قعر صينية نكون قد وضعنا بها باقي الزيت.

٦- عند امتلاء الصينية ندخلها الفرن لبضع دقائق وتقدم ساخنة.

Falafel

FRIED CHICKPEA BALLS

12 PIECES

Falafel is a very popular fast food dish in Lebanon. It is often served in warm bread with fresh and pickled vegetables and with tahini dressing. Falafel is also very popular in Egypt, where the ingredients differ slightly.

ABOUT 2 CUPS (400 G) DRIED CHICKPEAS
3⅕ CUPS (950 G) DRIED FAVA BEANS
¾ CUP (113 G) GRATED ONION
3 TABLESPOONS MINCED GARLIC
ABOUT 1 CUP (30 G) FINELY CHOPPED CORIANDER
1 TABLESPOON FINELY CHOPPED RED CHILI
SALT
CUMIN, CINNAMON, AND SUMAC ACCORDING TO TASTE
FRYING OIL
ABOUT 2 CUPS (288 G) SESAME SEEDS

1. Rinse the chickpeas and fava beans, and soak them in cold water for at least 12 hours. Rinse well, and allow them to drain.

2. Mix the chickpeas and fava beans in a food processor. Add onion, garlic, coriander, and chili. Mix a little bit longer. Add salt and the remaining spices according to your own preference. Allow the mixture to stand and swell for 2 hours.

3. Heat plenty of oil in a fryer or heavy–based saucepan. Shape small balls out of the falafel batter. Roll them in sesame seeds and fry in oil until they are golden brown. Dip a piece of bread in the oil to check if it is at the correct temperature.

4. Serve with tarator dressing (see recipe below) and fresh and pickled vegetables, preferably in pita bread.

TARATOR DRESSING

½–1 TEASPOON MINCED GARLIC
SALT
1 CUP (250 G) TAHINI
⅕ CUP (47 ML) WATER
¾ CUP (177 ML) JUICE OF LEMON OR ORANGE

1. Crush garlic with salt in a mortar.

2. Whisk the tahini and slowly add water while you beat the tahini.

3. Add the juice and stir. Add the salt and garlic paste into the dressing once it is smooth.

فلافل

عدد الحصص: ١٢ حبّة تقريبًا

فليفلة حرّة مفرومة ١ ملعقة كبيرة
فول مجروش ٤ أكواب
حمّص وسمسم ٢ كوب من كل صنف
بصل مفرومًا ناعمًا ٣/٤ الكوب
ثوم مدقوق ١/٤ كوب
كزبرة خضراء مفرومة ١ كوب
ملح، كمون، قرفة، سماق حسب الرغبة

١– يُنقى الفول المجروش والحمّص جيداً، ثم يغسلا وينقعا لفترة أقلها ١٢ ساعة، بالماء البارد، وإن استعمال البيكربونات في النقع هو أمر اختياري.

٢– بعد مرور هذه الفترة تضرب هذه الحبوب بعضها مع بعض في آلة الفرم، ويضاف إليها بعد ذلك البصل والثوم والكزبرة والفليفلة الحرّة، وتضرب من جديد بعضها مع بعض، وتضاف إليها البهارات وتترك لفترة ساعتين.

٣– نضع الزيت في طنجرة على النار، وبينما يحمى نضع أقراص الفلافل الخاصّة ونمررها على السمسم ثم نسقطها في الزيت ذي الحرارة المعتدلة.

٤– تقدم الفلافل مع الطراطور وتشكيلة من الخضار الطازجة كالبندورة والبقدونس والنعناع والفجل والبصل الأخضر، والكبيس على أنواعه من لفت وخيار وجزر وقرنبيط وغيرها حسب الرغبة.

صلصة الطراطور

١/٢ – ١ ملعقة ثوم مدقوق
ملح حسب الذوق
٢ ١/٢ ديسيلتر طحينة
١/٢ دسلتر ماء
٣/٤ ١ ديسيلتر عصير الليمون الحامض أو البرتقال

دقي الثوم مع الملح في هاون.
أخفقي الطحينة وأضيفي قليلاً من الماء شيئاً فشيئاً بينما أنت تخففين.
أضيفي العصير وخليط الملح والثوم وحركيه جيداً حين تكون الصلصة أصبحت مستوية ومختلطة مع بعضها بشكل جيد بحيث لا تكون مكوناتها مفصولة عن بعضها.

Kibbeh

Ground Meat Dishes

 وجبـات اللحـم المفـروم كبــة

Raw Kibbeh

LEBANESE STEAK TARTARE

10 SERVINGS (AS A STARTER)

An important element among Lebanon's cold meze dishes. There are many different recipes for this dish, and they all use various herbs. Traditionally the meat is mashed by hand; here we have chosen to use ground beef. Preferably, request to have the meat ground twice.

18 OUNCES (500 G) LAMB OR VEAL
9 OUNCES (250 G) CRUSHED WHEAT
SALT
1 TEASPOON CINNAMON
CHOPPED FRESH MINT LEAVES ACCORDING TO TASTE
CHOPPED FRESH BASIL LEAVES ACCORDING TO TASTE
1 SMALL YELLOW ONION, GRATED
PEEL OF 1 LEMON
OLIVE OIL

1. Mix ground meat with crushed wheat. Mix in a blender or a mortar.

2. Add spices, herbs, onion, and lemon zest, and work together into an even and smooth batter.

3. Place the ground meat on a platter, shape it, and cut patterns on the surface with a sharp knife. Garnish with extra mint leaves and onion wedges. Drizzle with olive oil.

الكبّة النيّة

عدد الحصص: ١٠ إذا قدّمت كمقبلات

تحتلّ الكبة النية مركزاً مهماً وأساسياً في المازه اللبنانية الباردة. تتعدّد وصفاتها من حيث المطيبات المستعملة بها إلا أن المكوّن الأساسي لها فهو اللحم، وتؤكل نيئة.

تحضّر الكبة النية في جميع الأقضية، وقد يكون مصدرها إما الخروف أو الماعز، وفي بعض الأحيان البقر إذا كان عجلاً بلدياً صغيرا. ويطيّب هذا اللحم بمطيبات مختلفة كالبصل المبشور والحبق وبرش الحامض والمردكوش أو أحدها فقط.

فيما يختصّ بالكبة النية التي اكتشفناها في الجنوب، في قضاء بنت جبيل وبالأخصّ في عيتا الشعب، فيُطلق عليها اسم الفراكة، وتصنع بمزج اللحم بالكمّونه. العنصر الآخر المهم جداً في الكبة النيّة إلى جانب المطيبات هو البرغل الناعم الرفيع الأسمر. أما إذا لم نستعمل البرغل، فنحصل على وصفة أخرى من وصفات المطبخ اللبناني الخاص بالمازات الباردة وهي التابلة أو الهبرة النيّة، والتي لا تقل أهمية من حيث النكهة والطعم.

ومن حيث المقادير، فلكلّ كيلو من اللحم المفروم ناعماً أو المدقوق في الجرن الحجري، نضيف، إلى جانب المطيبات، ما يعادل الـ ٤٠٠ إلى ٦٠٠ غرام من البرغل، وذلك بحسب الرغبة.

نباشر بدقّ اللحم في الجرن، وعندما يصبح ناعماً، نضيف إليه المطيبات ومن بعدها البرغل، ونستمرّ بالدق والتحريك حتى نحصل على مزيج واحد متماسك. تقدّم الكبة النيئة مزينة في (جاط) مع قبعات النعناع الأخضر، وشرائح البصل النيئة، ويُغمر سطحها بزيت الزيتون الطبيعي. وبعض الأشخاص قد يضيفون الصنوبر المنقوع وصلصة الثوم.

Kibbeh Mtabbaqah

KIBBEH PIE WITH FILLING

8–10 PORTIONS

In this recipe, both the pie shell and the filling contain kibbeh ground meat. The original recipe contains goat meat. We have replaced it with ground lamb.

PIE SHELL
ABOUT 3⅕ CUPS (450 G) FINE BULGUR
ABOUT 2 POUNDS (900 G) GROUND LAMB
1 GRATED YELLOW ONION
SALT AND PEPPER

FILLING
1⅓ CUPS (300 G) BUTTER
ABOUT 1 CUP (150 G) CHOPPED ONION
ABOUT 12 OUNCES (350 G) GROUND LAMB, PREFERABLY COARSELY
　　GROUND
½ TABLESPOON NUTMEG
½ TABLESPOON CARDAMOM
1 PIECE OF MASTIC (OPTIONAL)
⅕ CUP (27 G) PINE NUTS

1. Begin with the pie shell: Rinse and soak the bulgur grains for 10 minutes. Drain and mix with ground lamb and onions. Mix well; the batter should be as smooth as possible. Season with salt and pepper.

2. Make the filling: Melt the butter in a saucepan and fry the onion without darkening it. Add the minced lamb and spices.

3. Fry the ground meat with onions until it is thoroughly cooked. Add pine nuts and stir fry them until they turn golden brown.

4. Grease a round baking pan.

5. Cover the bottom of the mold with half of the batter for the shell and spread the filling on top.

6. Cover with the remaining batter and cut a pattern on the surface with a sharp knife. Place little pieces of butter on top.

7. Bake at 350°F (175°C) until the surface has a beautiful color.

8. Allow to cool slightly and cut into diamond shapes before serving.

الكبّة المطبّقة

عدد الحصص: ٨-١٠

الكبة:
لحم ماعز ١ كيلو
برغل أبيض رفيع ٤٠٠ / ٥٠٠ غرام
بصل مجروش ناعم ١ حبة
ملح وبهار حسب الرغبة

الحشو :
لحم ماعز مفروم خشن ٣٠٠ غرام
صنوبر ١/٢ كوب
بصل مفروم ناعم ١ كوب
بهارات
(جوزة الطيب، حب الهال، مستكة) ١ ملعقة كبيرة
سمنة ٢ كوب

١- نحضّر الكبة كما في وصفة الكبة الزغرتاوية.

٢- لتحضير الحشوة، نذوّب كوباً من السمنة في وعاء على النار، ونضيف إليه البصل المفروم الناعم، ثم اللحم المفروم الخشن والبهارات.

٣- نُقلّب مواد الحشوة على النار حتى ينضج اللحم، ثم نضيف إليها الصنوبر.

٤- ندهن أرض وجوانب صينية الخَبيز بالقليل من السمنة.

٥- نوزّع ونبسط نصف كمية الكبة في قعر الصينية.

٦- نضع طبقة الحشوة عليها ثم نغطيها بالنصف المتبقي من الكبة.

٧- نقلّم وجه الصينية بالسكين ومن ثم نوزّع ما تبقى من كمية السمنة على وجه الصينية.

٨- نخبزها في فرن متوسط الحرارة إلى أن يحمرّ سطحها. وتقدّم.

Kibbeh with Fish

LEBANESE FISH PIE

6–8 PORTIONS

Kibbeh comes in all shapes and forms. Made with fish, it is one of Lebanon's most famous coastal dishes.

3 CUPS (420 G) FINE BULGUR
ABOUT 2 POUNDS (900 G) WHITE FISH FILLET, MINCED
⅕ CUP (6 G) CHOPPED PARSLEY LEAVES
⅕ CUP (6 G) CORIANDER LEAVES
⅕ CUP (30 G) YELLOW ONION, FINELY CHOPPED
PEEL OF 1 LEMON
SALT
⅔ CUP (95 ML) OLIVE OIL
3 CUPS (450 G) SLICED YELLOW ONIONS
1 TABLESPOON TURMERIC
ABOUT 1 CUP (135 G) PINE NUTS
BUTTER

1. Rinse the bulgur grains and drain them. Use your palms to squeeze out all the liquid.

2. Combine bulgur, minced fish, parsley, coriander, finely chopped onions, grated lemon peel, and salt. Set aside for now.

3. Heat the oil in a frying pan, and fry the sliced onion until it becomes translucent.

4. Add the turmeric and stir well.

5. Add the pine nuts, and stir until they are mixed with the onions without burning them.

6. Cover the bottom of a pie dish, about 12 inches (30 cm) in diameter, with the onion blend.

7. Pinch off small pieces of minced fish, and flatten them between your palms. Layer them on top of the onion blend. Continue until the entire surface is covered.

8. Cut a decorative pattern with a sharp knife. Add a bit of butter, and place in the oven at 350°F (175°C).

9. The *kibbeh* is done when the surface is golden brown. Cut into triangles and serve.

Tip!

You can also cover the bottom of the pie with a layer of minced fish, then add a layer of the onion blend, and finish off with a layer of minced fish, to get a pie like in the picture.

كبة السمك

عدد الحصص: ٦-٨

من أشهر الوصفات البحرية في لبنان، وصفة كبة السمك التي تنافس الصيادية والسمكة الحرّة على المرتبة الأولى بين الأطعمة. ففكرة الكبة امتدّت لتصل إلى الأسماك، والبدأ نفسه، أي مزج البرغل الناعم مع صنف اللحم المستعمل. وقد يكون لحماً أحمر (بقر أو غنم) أو أبيض (دجاج أو سمك). أما وجود هذا الطبق على المائدة اللبنانية فمهمّ جداً، لأنه يُعطي مستوىً رفيعاً لكل لائحة الطعام المقدّمة.

فيليه سمك أبيض مطحون ١ كيلو
برغل ناعم أبيض ٣ أكواب
بصل مفروم فرماً ناعماً ١/٢ كوب
بصل مقطّع إلى جوانح ٣ أكواب
بقدونس مفروم ناعم ١/٤ كوب
كزبرة مفرومة ناعمة ١/٤ كوب
بشارة قشر الحامض ١ حبة
زيت زيتون ١/٢ كوب
صنوبر ١ كوب
ملح حسب الرغبة
عقدة صفراء ١ ملعقة كبيرة

١- يصوّل البرغل وذلك بغسله وتصفيته، ومن ثم عصره، بوضعه بين الكفين والضغط جيداً.

٢- نخلط البرغل مع السمك المطحون، البقدونس، الكزبرة، البصل المفروم ناعماً والملح وبشارة قشر الحامض.

٣- نضع زيت الزيتون في مقلاة على النار حتى يحمى، ثم نضيف إليه البصل المقطع إلى جوانح.

٤- نباشر بالتحريك حتى يصبح البصل شفافاً، فنوزّع عليه العقدة الصفراء ونعاود التحريك.

٥- نضيف بعدها الصنوبر، ونقلّب المواد بعضها ببعض حتى تختلط جيداً، ولا نترك الصنوبر يتلوّن.

٦- نطفئ النار ونوزّع المواد، مع الزيت، في كعب صينية مستديرة، قطرها ٣٠ سنتم تقريباً.

٧- نأخذ قطعة صغيرة من كبة السمك، ونضغط عليها بين الكفين حتى تصبح متوسطة السماكة، ونضعها فوق قلية البصل والصنوبر، وهكذا دواليك حتى نغطي كل القلية الموزّعة في الصينية.

٨- نزيّن سطح الكبة بالسكين، وندخلها فرناً متوسط الحرارة مع القليل من المواد الدهنية على سطحها.

٩- حين تصبح الكبة ذهبية اللون تكون قد نضجت، تقدّم مقطعة إلى مثلثات متشابهة الحجم.

١٠- هنالك مَن يضع كمية من الكبة في الأسفل أي في قعر الصينية، والحشوة عليها، ومن ثم تغطى هذه الأخيرة بطبقة من الكبة، فتشبه عندها وصفة الكبة بالصينية.

Kibbeh from Iraq

SERVES 4

This kibbeh recipe comes from Mosul, a city in Iraq.

Filling

18 OUNCES (500 G) GROUND LAMB
OLIVE OIL
2 TABLESPOONS WATER
2 LARGE YELLOW ONIONS
⅔ CUP (43 G) CHOPPED ALMONDS
⅔ CUP (58 G) RAISINS
SALT
BLACK PEPPER

Pie shell

2 CUPS (280 G) COARSE BULGUR
ABOUT 1 CUP (140 G) FINE BULGUR WHEAT, OR SEMOLINA
8⅘ OUNCES (250 G) FINELY GROUND BEEF

1. Begin by making the filling: Fry the ground lamb in oil. Add water and the finely chopped onions. Sauté until the onions turn translucent. Add the almonds, raisins, salt, and pepper. Set aside and allow to cool.

2. Make the pie shell: Rinse the bulgur grains and squeeze out the liquid. Mix the two kinds of bulgur with the ground beef. Add a little bit of water if it gets too dry. Work into a dough and shape into two balls. Roll out the dough to form two circles on parchment paper. Spread the filling on top of one of the circles, place the other on top, and pinch at the edges.

3. Gently place the *kibbeh* in a large pot with simmering water for 5 to 10 minutes. Drain before serving.

الكبّة العراقية

من مدينة الموصل

المقادير
٢ كوب برغل ناعم
كوب جريش أو صريصرة، أي البرغل البودرة (وإذا لم يتوفر يستبدل بالسميد ولكن حينها ستختلف النتيجة النهائية قليلاً).
١/٤ كيلو لحم بقر
١/٢ كيلو لحم غنم
٢ بصلة كبيرة
١/٢ كوب لوز وزبيب
ملح وفلفل أسود حسب الرغبة

طريقة التحضير :

١– يفرم لحم الغنم ناعمًا ويقلى في الدهن ويضاف إليه قليل من الماء ثم يضاف إليه البصل المفروم ويقلّب معه على النار حتى ينضج ثم يضاف اللوز المقشر والمقطع بالطول والزبيب ويتبل بالملح والفلفل ويترك ليبرد.

٢– ينقى البرغل والجريش ويفضل عدم غسل البرغل إلا إذا احتاج الأمر لذلك إذ يجب حينها غسله بسرعة وعصره جيدًا للتخلص من الماء.

٣– يفرم لحم البقر ويدق في الهاون(جرن) حتى يصبح ناعمًا ثم يمزج مع البرغل والجريش ونعاود الدق حتى يصبح عجينة متماسكة ويرش البرغل بقليل من الماء البارد أثناء الدق وخاصة إذ كان غير مغسول.

٤– نستخرج الكريات من هذه العجينة ونعطي كل واحدة منها شكلاً دائريًا.

٥– نضع بعضًا من حشوة اللحمة على أعلى القطعة ونغطيها بقطعة ثانية مستعينين بورق النايلون للتمكن من رفعها ووضعها على الدائرة الأولى.

٦– تلحم الأطراف ببعضها البعض ثم يسلق القرص النهائي ويقدم.

Rice Kibbeh from Iraq

RICE BALLS WITH GROUND MEAT FILLING

ABOUT 20 PIECES

Stuffed rice balls come in many different variations. You can also boil potatoes or lentils with rice or mix the egg directly into the rice.

2 CUPS (380 G) ROUND-GRAIN RICE
ABOUT 4¼ CUPS (1 LITER) WATER
1 TABLESPOON TURMERIC
18 OUNCES (500 G) GROUND LAMB
A TOTAL OF ⅔ CUP (43 G) BLANCHED ALMONDS
  (OR PINE NUTS) AND RAISINS, MIXED
1 SMALL CELERY
SALT AND PEPPER
OPTIONAL: CINNAMON AND NUTMEG
1 EGG
FRYING OIL

1. Rinse the rice and cook it gently in water with turmeric.

2. Pour out any excess liquid.

3. Place the rice in a bowl and work it with your hands until it becomes like a dough.

4. Mix the ground lamb with the chopped almonds (or whole pine nuts), raisins, and chopped celery. Season with salt and pepper, and possibly cinnamon and nutmeg.

5. Moisten your hands with water and shape balls out of the rice. Make a hole at one end with a finger and fill it with a little bit of the ground meat blend. Seal the hole and shape into an oval ball with two pointed ends.

6. Brush with beaten egg, and fry a few at a time in the oil until they turn beautifully golden brown.

كبّة الأرزّ العراقية

رزّ مصري ٢ كوب
لحمة مفرومة ناعمة ٥٠٠ غرام
لحمة هبرة ١ كيلو
بصل مفروم ناعم ٢ كوب
سمنة ١ كوب
صنوبر ١ كوب
قرفة، جوزة الطيب، بهار حسب الرغبة
ملح حسب الرغبة

١- يُنقّى الأرزّ ويُغسل، ثم ينقع بالماء الفاتر لمدّة نصف ساعة.

٢- يُصفّى بعد ذلك ويدقّ ناعماً.

٣- نضع ملعقتين إلى ثلاث من السمنة، في وعاء على النار، وعندما تذوب وتحمى، نضيف إليها كوباً من البصل المفروم حتى يذبل، فنضيف الصنوبر، ثم اللحمة المفرومة ناعماً.

٤- تطحن بهذا الوقت اللحمة الهبرة، مع ما تبقّى من بصل مفروم ناعم، حتى نحصل على عجينة ناعمة.

٥- نضيف إليها الأرزّ المطحون، والبهارات، والملح، ونجبلها باليد.

٦- ندهن بنصف كمية السمنة المتبقية كعبّ وجوانبَ صينية الخبيز، ونمدّ بكعبها نصف عجينة اللحمة/الأرز.

٧- نوزّع عليها قليّة اللحمة والصنوبر، ثم نغطيها بالنصف الثاني من عجينة اللحمة/الأرز.

٨- يصقل سطح الصينية، ثم يزيّن بالسكين بمثل تقطيع البقلاوة، ونوزّع ما تبقّى من سمنة عليها، ونخبزها بالفرن حتى الاستواء الكامل.

Vegetarian Kibbeh with Onion and Pine Nut Filling

SERVES 4

Pine nuts often appear in Lebanese cuisine. Here they end up in a vegetarian version of kibbeh.

3 CUPS (420 G) FINE BULGUR
2½ CUPS (540 G) OLIVE OIL
1½ CUPS (153 G) GRAHAM FLOUR
SALT AND PEPPER
6½ TABLESPOONS DRIED MINT
1½ CUPS (225 G) GRATED YELLOW ONION
2 CUPS (473 G) WATER
3⅗ CUPS (570 G) SLICED YELLOW ONIONS
1½ CUPS (200 G) PINE NUTS
VEGETABLE OIL FOR FRYING

1. Begin by making the *kibbeh* batter. Mix the bulgur with 1 cup of the olive oil, then add the flour, salt, pepper, mint, grated onion, and water. Mix well.

2. Heat the remaining oil in a saucepan. Fry the sliced onions until they turn soft and translucent.

3. Remove the onion from the pan and allow it to drain on paper towels. Fry the pine nuts golden brown in the same oil. Remove and drain on paper towels. Mix the onion with the nuts.

4. Shape the *kibbeh* batter into round balls and make a hole in the middle of each ball. Fill the holes with the onion and pine nut blend, and seal the hole. Fry a few balls at a time in the hot oil until they turn golden brown.

5. Serve the balls warm or at room temperature.

كبة نباتية
بحشوة البصل والصنوبر

عدد الحصص: ٦ حبّات صغيرة

برغل ناعم ٣ أكواب
طحين القمح ١/٢ ١ كوب
زيت زيتون ١/٢ ٢ كوب
ملح، بهار حسب الرغبة
نعناع يابس ١/٢ كوب
بصل مبروش ١/٢ ١ كوب
بصل مقطع جوانح ٤ أكواب
صنوبر بلدي ١/٢ ١ كوب
ماء ٢ كوب تقريباً

١- نفرك البرغل بكوب واحد من زيت الزيتون، ثم نضيف إليه الطحين والملح والبهار والنعناع اليابس والبصل (المبروش) والماء، وندعك المواد حتى نحصل على عجينة متماسكة.

٢- نضع ما تبقّى من زيت الزيتون في وعاء على النار حتى يحمى، فنضيف إليه البصل الجوانح، ونقلّب حتى يُصبح شفافا.

٣- نصفّي البصل من الزيت برفعه من الوعاء بواسطة ملعقة مخرّمة ووضعه جانبا، ثم نضيف الى الزيت نفسه الصنوبر لنحمّره، بعدها نصفّيه بدوره ونرفعه من الزيت.

٤- تقرّص العجينة مثل الكبة التي رأيناها في إهدن -زغرتا، وتُحشى بالبصل والصنوبر وتُقلى بالزيت العميق، وتقدّم.

Shish Barak Kibbeh

LEBANESE RAVIOLI WITH CORIANDER AND YOGURT SAUCE

6 SERVINGS

Shish Barak is Lebanon's answer to ravioli. It is often served with yogurt and plenty of coriander.

2 CUPS (473 ML) FLOUR

⅖ CUP (95 ML) WATER

6 TABLESPOONS VEGETABLE OIL

5.3 OUNCES (150 G) FINELY GROUND LAMB

SALT

3 TABLESPOONS SLICED ONION

2 TABLESPOONS MINCED GARLIC

ABOUT 1 CUP (200 G) COOKED CHICKPEAS (OR CANNED)

10.6 OUNCES (300 G) LAMB MEAT IN SMALL CUBES

ABOUT 2 CUPS (60 G) CHOPPED CORIANDER LEAVES

1 CUP (237 ML) BEEF STOCK

ABOUT 4¼ CUPS (1 L) PLAIN YOGURT

⅖ CUP (51 G) CORNSTARCH

3 TABLESPOONS WHOLE PINE NUTS

12 HOLLOW KIBBEH, SEE KIBBEH MKABKABEH ON PAGE 34

1. Mix flour with water and a tablespoon of oil. Work together into a dough. Roll out the dough and cut out circles, about 2 inches (5 cm) in diameter. Place a little bit of ground lamb and salt on each circle and pinch into small bundles, so-called *shish barak*.

2. Put them on a greased baking sheet and bake in the oven at 400°F (200°C) until they are golden brown.

3. Heat 3 tablespoons of oil in a saucepan over medium heat. Fry the onion until it has become translucent and soft. Add half of the garlic.

4. Add the drained chickpeas and the diced lamb a few minutes later. Cover with a lid and simmer.

5. Pour half the coriander along with the broth after 10 minutes. Remove the lid and continue to simmer.

6. When about a quarter of the broth has evaporated, add the yogurt and stir.

7. Mix the cornstarch in 1 cup of cold water and pour a little bit at a time into the yogurt blend while stirring, until the sauce is moderately thick. Season with salt.

8. Heat 2 tablespoons of oil and fry the other half of the coriander leaves with the rest of the garlic and pine nuts.

9. Serve the *shish barak* bundles with yogurt sauce, rice, and *kibbe*h (i.e., *kibbeh mkabkabeh*). Garnish with the coriander blend. You can also place the bundles in the sauce.

كبة شيش برك

عدد الحصص: ٦

زيت نباتي ١ كوب

بصل مفروم جوانح ٣ ملاعق كبيرة

ثوم مدقوق ٦ ملاعق صغيرة

حمص حب مسلوق ١ كوب

كزبرة مفرومة ٢ كوب

مكعبات اللحم ٣٥٠ غرام

مرقة عظام الغنم ١ كوب

لبن ٨ أكواب

نشاء (إختياري) ١/٢ كوب

طحين ٢ كوب

لحم مفروم ناعم ١ كوب

أقراص كبة فارغة ١٢قرصاً

صنوبر ٣ ملاعق كبيرة

ملح حسب الرغبة

١- نضيف نصف كوب من الماء إلى الطحين ونخلطهما بملعقة كبيرة من الزيت ثم نرقّ العجينة ونقطعها إلى دوائر صغيرة، ونحشو كل دائرة بالقليل من اللحمة المفرومة، ثم نقفل الدائرة حتى نحصل على كريات صغيرة. ونستطيع استبدال هذه الحشوة بالكفتة.

٢- نضع الكريات في صينية الفرن وندخلها على نار متوسطة الحرارة حتى تشقر من الخارج. وكان باستطاعتنا سلقها أو قليها.

٣- نضع ٣ ملاعق كبيرة من الزيت في طنجرة على النار. وعندما يحمى، نضيف إليه البصل ونصف كمية الثوم المدقوق.

٤- بعد بضع دقائق نضيف الحمص المسلوق ومكعبات اللحم، ونضع غطاء على الطنجرة لاستخراج أقصى كمية من خواص اللحم. وكان باستطاعتنا سلق اللحم جانباً.

٥- بعد مرور حوالى عشر دقائق، نضيف نصف كمية الكزبرة، ونقلب المواد بعضها مع البعض الآخر ثم نضيف المرقة.

٦- بعد مرور بضع دقائق، نرى أنّ المرقة قد انخفض مستواها قليلاً، فنضيف اللبن ونحرّك.

٧- يُذوّب النشاء بالماء البارد ويُضاف على مهل إلى اللبن، دون التوقف عن التحريك.

٨- تحضر الكبة أقراصاً بعجن البرغل جيداً على اليد، ثم إضافته إلى اللحم لنحصل على تكوين أفضل. نأخذ عندها من العجينة كريات صغيرة، ونعطيها شكل الأقراص مثلما رأينا في إهدن، قضاء زغرتا.

٩- تسلق الكبة وتضاف مع البرك المشوية إلى الصلصة التي اشتدّت تحت تأثير النشاء. وتقلى بقايا الكزبرة مع الثوم والصنوبر بملعقتين كبيرتين من الزيت. وعند التقديم، تزيّن هذه القلية سطح الصلصة. ويُقدّم هذا الطبق مع الأرز الأبيض المفلفل.

Main Courses

وجبات ساخنة

Freekeh with Chicken

ROASTED GREEN WHEAT WITH CHICKEN

SERVES 4

Freekeh is roasted green wheat that looks sort of like green rice. You can replace it with bulgur, brown rice, or wheat berries.

1 WHOLE CHICKEN
4¼ CUPS (1 L) CHICKEN STOCK
2 BAY LEAVES
2 PIECES OF MASTIC (RESIN, CAN BE OMITTED)
2 TABLESPOONS BUTTER
4½ CUPS (1 L) *freekeh* (ROASTED GREEN WHEAT), OR
    WHEAT BERRIES, BROWN RICE, OR BULGUR
GROUND CARDAMOM
CINNAMON
CUMIN
BLACK PEPPER
3 TABLESPOONS PINE NUTS
3 TABLESPOONS BLANCHED AND PEELED ALMONDS
3 TABLESPOONS PISTACHIOS

1. Let the chicken simmer in the chicken broth, bay leaves, and mastic until completely cooked. It takes about 1 hour. Then place the chicken on a baking tray and place it in the oven under the grill heater until it gets a nice color. Save the broth.

2. Melt the butter in a saucepan over medium heat. Add the rinsed and drained wheat.

3. Add spices according to taste and stir for a few minutes.

4. Pour the broth over the wheat until it is completely covered.

5. Bring the broth to a boil, cover with a lid, and reduce the heat. Simmer until the wheat has softened but is still juicy.

6. Meanwhile, roast the pine nuts and the almonds in a dry, large frying pan. Serve the chicken on a bed of *freekeh* and decorate with pistachios, almonds, and pine nuts.

الفريكة بالدجاج

دجاج مقطع إلى ٨ قطع ١ (١٤٥٠ غرام)
قمح فريك ومرقة دجاج ٤ أكواب من كل صنف
سمنة ٢ ملعقة كبيرة
ورق غار ومستكة ٢ حبة من كل صنف
حب الهال مطحون، قرفة رشة من كل صنف
كمّون وبهار أسود وكراوية رشة من كل صنف
صنوبر ولوز مسلوق ومقشر ٣ ملاعق كبيرة من كل صنف

١- نضع قطع الدجاج في المرقة على النار حتى تنضج ثم نخرجها من المرقة ونضعها في صينية بالفرن حتى تحمّر.

٢- نضع السمنة في طنجرة على نار متوسطة الحرارة، وعندما تذوب نضيف إليها القمح المغسول جيدًا ليجفّ ماؤه.

٣- نضيف البهارات كلها، ولا نتوقف عن التحريك لبضع دقائق.

٤- نغمر القمح بالمرقة التي ازدادت نكهتها بعد أن سلقنا قطع الدجاج بداخلها.

٥- عندما تبدأ المرقة بالغليان نضع غطاء على الطنجرة ونخفّف النار حتى ينضج القمح. كما نستطيع وضع الطنجرة بالفرن لمدّة ٢٥ دقيقة.

٦- أنصح بترك القليل من المرقة في القمح وإلّا جفّ كثيرًا.

٧- بينما القمح في الفرن، نقلي الصنوبر واللوز، وعند السكب نضع فوق القمح قطع الدجاج المحمّرة والصنوبر واللوز..

Kaftah with Pine Nuts

BEEF PATTIES WITH PINE NUTS

6 SERVINGS

This is one of my favorite dishes from the region of Aley, probably because I used to spend my summers there as a child. It contains a lot of pine nuts, but also mountain tomatoes, which are very common in this region.

5 TABLESPOONS BUTTER

3 CUPS (400 G) PINE NUTS

1 POUND (450 G) GROUND LAMB OR GROUND BEEF

3⅘ CUPS (115 G) CHOPPED FLAT-LEAF PARSLEY

2 YELLOW ONIONS, FINELY CHOPPED

SALT AND PEPPER

4 CUPS (600 G) SLICED ONION

3 CUPS (500 G) FREEKEH (ROASTED GREEN WHEAT, CAN
    BE REPLACED WITH WHEAT BERRIES), OR 6 POTATOES

CUMIN AND CARDAMOM

SALT

ABOUT 1½ CUPS (400 G) CRUSHED TOMATOES
    (OR 4 LARGE, FRESH AND PEELED TOMATOES)

1 TABLESPOON TOMATO PUREE

ABOUT 2 CUPS (473 ML) WATER

1. Heat the butter in a skillet, and sauté the pine nuts until they get a little bit of color. Drain and set aside.

2. Mix ground beef, parsley, and onions with salt and pepper. Chop or mix everything one more time and mix again. Shape into small patties and fill them with pine nuts. Sauté in the butter and set aside.

3. Heat up half of the used butter and pour it over the onions in a saucepan along with the *freekeh*, or peeled and sliced potatoes, cumin, cardamom, and salt.

4. Add the tomatoes.

5. Dilute the tomato paste with water and pour it into the skillet.

6. Bring to a boil and add the beef patties. Cook until the *freekeh* or potatoes are soft. If necessary, add more diluted tomato paste.

كفتة بالهينية

عدد الحصص: ٦

لحمة هبرة ١ كيلو

ليّة غنم ١٠٠ غرام

بصل ٣ حبات

بطاطا ٣ حبات

بندورة كاملة ٦ حبات

بندورة مقطعة شرحات مقدار ٣ حبات أيضاً

ربّ البندورة ٢ ملعقة كبيرة

سمنة ٣ ملاعق كبيرة

ملح حسب الرغبة

١- تطحن اللحمة طحناً ناعماً وتخلط مع الأليّه التي تطحن بدورها، ويُضاف الملح حسب الذوق والرغبة.

٢- تقرّص العجينة إلى أحجام متوسطة ومتشابهة، وتحمّر بالسمنة الحامية، ثم تصفّى جيداً وتوضع جانباً.

٣- نسلق البندورة في ماء يغلي لمدّة ثلاث دقائق من بدء الغليان، ثم نقشرها ونطحن اللبّ ليصبح عصيراً.

٤- نقشر البصل والبطاطا ونقطعها شرحات.

٥- نوزّع أقراص الكفتة في صينية، ثم ندخلها فرناً متوسط الحرارة، ونغطيها بشرحات البصل، فالبطاطا، وأخيراً البندورة.

٦- نذوّب ربّ البندورة في عصير البندورة مع القليل من الملح، ونوزّعه في الصينية.

٧- تقدّم مباشرة عند النضوج التام لكافة المواد. ومن الممكن إعطاء أشكال مختلفة للبطاطا مثل الشكل المستدير أو المستطيل بدلاً من الشرحات التقليدية، كما يمكن تزيينها بالصنوبر والبقدونس المفروم ناعما.

Arabic Stew with Green Beans

6 SERVINGS

Beirut is often referred to as "Paris of the Middle East," and sometimes the food there is very similar to French cuisine. This is an Arabic variation of a classic French meat stew.

ABOUT 5 CUPS (900 G) GREEN BEANS, SUCH AS STRING BEANS
1 TABLESPOON BUTTER
1⅕ CUPS (270 G) FINELY CHOPPED YELLOW ONION
ABOUT 12 OUNCES (350 G) STEWED PIECES OF BEEF, SUCH AS PRIME RIB
3 DICED TOMATOES
2 CUPS (473 ML) WATER
1 TEASPOON TOMATO PUREE
SALT

1. Clean the beans, remove the "string," rinse, and set aside.

2. Heat the butter in a pan and sauté the chopped onion and stewed pieces.

3. Add the beans once the meat is browned. Stir for a few minutes, then add the tomatoes. Put the lid on and simmer for a few minutes.

4. Remove the lid and add the water, tomato purée, and salt. Boil slowly over medium heat until the meat is cooked.

5. Serve warm with rice or noodles.

يخنة اللوبياء باللحمة

عدد الحصص: ٦

لوبياء بادرية ١ كيلو
لحمة رأس عصفور (موزات) ٣٠٠ غرام
بندورة مقطعة مربعات ٣ حبات
بصل مفروم ناعم ١ كوب
سمنة عربية ١ ملعقة كبيرة
رب البندورة ١ ملعقة صغيرة
ماء ٢ كوب
ملح حسب الرغبة

١- نقمّع اللوبياء، ونغسلها، ونضعها جانباً.

٢- نضع السمنة في طنجرة على النار، وعندما تذوب وتحمى نضيف إليها البصل المفروم ناعماً، وعندما يصبح شفافاً، نضيف اللحمة المقطعة إلى رأس عصفور.

٣- تقلّب اللحمة جيدا، ثم نضيف اللوبياء، نحرك المواد بعضها مع بعض، لبضع الوقت، ثم نضيف البندورة، ثم نضع غطاء على الوعاء، ونتركه على النار.

٤- بعد مرور بضع دقائق، نرفع الغطاء ونضع الماء فوق الوصفة، ورب البندورة، والملح، ثم نتركها على نار متوسطة حتى النضوج الكامل.

٥- يقدّم هذا الطبق ساخنا، وبجانبه الأرز بالشعيرية.

Molokhiya from Deyrintar

ROYAL CHICKEN DISH FROM THE SOUTH OF LEBANON

6 SERVINGS

Molokhiya is a leaf plant of the mallow genus that is well liked throughout Lebanon. The word means "royal" and is also the name of this dish. In the United States, we can substitute it for spinach or chard. This is how you cook it in the city of Deir Intar.

1 WHOLE CHICKEN
⅕ CUP (47 ML) VEGETABLE OIL
4 TABLESPOONS MINCED GARLIC
5 CUPS (155 G) CHOPPED CORIANDER LEAVES
ABOUT 10 CUPS (300 G) WHOLE MOLOKHIA, SPINACH, OR CHARD

DRESSING

1 YELLOW ONION, FINELY CHOPPED
⅖ CUP (95 ML) LEMON JUICE, OR WHITE WINE VINEGAR
SALT ACCORDING TO TASTE

1. Cook the chicken in water for about 1 hour, and skim off the fat from the surface at regular intervals. Save the broth.

2. Heat the oil in a pan and fry the garlic and coriander.

3. Add approximately 4 cups (1 liter) of the chicken stock. Bring to a boil and add the greens. Lastly, add the boned chicken.

4. Make the dressing. Serve alongside the chicken together with the rice.

اللوخية

عدد الحصص: ٣

وصفة مصرية أو لبنانية؟ لم نستطع الإجابة عن هذا السؤال. هل أدخلتها العائلات اللبنانية معها من مصر مثلما أدخلوا المغربية من شمال أفريقيا؟ يبقى الجواب عن هذه الأسئلة غير واضح. ولكن الواضح والأكيد أنّ الملوخية من أهم الوصفات اللبنانية، اشتهرت في الساحل والجنوب وامتدت إلى كافّة الأرجاء.

كل بيت في لبنان يحفظ «مونته» من الملوخية مجففة أو مجلّدة، لطبخها وتقديمها في فصل الشتاء.

رأيتها تحضّر في دير إنطار، قضاء بنت جبيل، على طريقة مشابهة للطريقة المصرية، أي بالورق الطويل. ورأيتها معلقة في كيس أبيض تُجفّف تحت الكرمة في قرية ليسا، قضاء جبيل. وجدت في صغبين، قضاء البقاع الغربي، نبتة تنافسها، اسمها الميتة، التي يبحث عنها اللبنانيون المغتربون في الولايات المتحدة، لتوافرها هناك، بعكس الملوخية، ولنكهتها القريبة منها.

وإني أنتظر بفارغ الصبر عندما أزور أهلي، وتكون والدتي قد حضّرت الملوخية على طريقتها الفريدة.

فتعالوا نكتشف معاً وصفة أم رئيف.

زيت نباتي ٢ كوب
ثوم مدقوق ٦ ملاعق كبيرة
كزبرة خضراء مفرومة ناعماً ٨ أكواب
فروج ١
ملوخية خضراء مفرومة ناعماً ١ كيلو

١– نضع الفروج في الماء البارد في وعاء على النار، وعندما يبدأ بالغليان، نلاحظ ظهور رغوة صفراء اللون على سطح الماء، فنزيلها ونستمر على هذا المنوال حتى تتوقف عن الظهور.

٢– نضيف عندها باقة من الأعشاب المطيّبة (كراث، كرفس، جزر، بقدونس، زعتر أخضر، حبق، عود قرفة)، ويُترك الفروج على النار حتى ينضج.

٣– نخرج الفروج من المرقة ونستخرج اللحم، ونصفّي المرقة.

٤– نضع نصف كمية الزيت في وعاء على النار، وعندما يحمى، نضيف إليه نصف كمية الثوم المدقوق.

٥– بعد بضع دقائق من التحريك، نضيف أيضاً نصف كمية الكزبرة، ونباشر بالتحريك حتى ينخفض حجم الكزبرة. عندها، نغمر الكلّ بمرقة الدجاج.

٦– نضع بهذا الوقت ما تبقى من الزيت في مقلاة على النار حتى يحمى، ونضيف ما تبقى من الثوم، ومن بعده بدقائق، ما تبقى من كزبرة.

٧– نباشر بالتحريك، وعندما تصل المرقة إلى درجة الغليان، نضيف إليها محتوى المقلاة الساخن.

٨– من أسرار نجاح الملوخية العديدة هو أن تكون كمية الملوخية مطابقة لكمية المرقة. فإذا كانت أقلّ تصبح الوصفة «صايتة»، أي سائلة كثيرا. وإذا كانت أكثر، تغدو «صلبة»، أي شديدة.

٩– عند أول الغليان، «نُسقّط» الملوخية في المرقة، نحرّكها، ونتركها على نار متوسطة حتى تنضج.

Shish Taouk

MARINATED CHICKEN SKEWERS

4–6 PORTIONS

This dish is one of the best dishes from the Ottoman Empire. The secret behind the juicy chicken is the marinade. It is the mother of all marinades.

⅖ CUP (50 G) MINCED GARLIC
2 TABLESPOONS MUSTARD
⅖ CUP (95 ML) LEMON JUICE
3 CUPS (710 ML) OLIVE OIL OR VEGETABLE OIL
1 TABLESPOON TOMATO PUREE
⅖ CUP (12 G) FRESH THYME
1 WHOLE CHICKEN

1. Mix the garlic, mustard, and lemon juice. Then add the oil, little by little, until you get a creamy dressing.

2. Add the tomato puree and thyme.

3. Remove the skin and bones from the chicken and cut it into pieces. Soak the poultry in the marinade, preferably overnight.

4. Thread the chicken pieces on wooden or metal skewers. You can also thread pieces of pepper and whole mushrooms in between the chicken pieces.

5. Barbeque or grill, or cook in the oven.

   Serve with a good aioli, lettuce, and potatoes.

شيش طاووق

عدد الحصص: ٣

من أطيب الوصفات اللبنانية التي ورثناها عن الاحتلال العثماني. أصبح اليوم الشيش طاووق العنصر الأساسي في جاط المشاوي. يرتكز تحضيره على نقع مكعبات الدجاج، مما يعطيها في اليوم التالي طراوة ونكهة. وأعتقد أنّ العثمانيين، من خلال الشيش طاووق والشاورما، أدخلوا فكرة النقع إلى المطبخ اللبناني. وإذا بحثنا في وصفاتنا، رأينا أنّ النقّع طبّق على هاتين الوصفتين، ثم امتدّ إلى لحم الطرائد، كالأرانب والغزلان التي كنا نراها في غاباتنا.

دجاج ١ (١٤٥٠ غرام)
ثوم مدقوق ١/٢ كوب
خردل ٢ ملعقة كبيرة
ربّ البندورة ١ ملعقة كبيرة
زيت زيتون أو نباتي ٣ أكواب
حامض ١/٢ كوب
زعتر أخضر منقّى ١/٢ كوب

١- يخفق الثوم مع الخردل، والحامض، والزيت، حتى نحصل على صلصة بكثافة المرهم.

٢- نضيف إليها ربّ البندورة والزعتر الأخضر.

٣- يسحّب الفروج من عظمه وجلده، ويقطع مكعبات متوسطة ومتشابهة الحجم.

٤- نضع الدجاج المقطع في النقيع وندخل الجاط إلى البراد، ويستحسن أن نبقيه طوال الليل قبل تحضيره.

٥- على عيدان من خشب أو حديد، تُشك اللحمة مع قطع الفيفلة الخضراء والفطر الحب، ونشويها على الفحم، أو في صينية بداخل الفرن.

Kofta Kebab

MINCED MEAT SKEWERS

4–6 PORTIONS

We make sure to use as high a temperature as possible when grilling meat to give it a nice, grilled surface so that it retains its natural juices inside. Meze dishes are usually followed by skewers with various kinds of grilled meats, such as kofta—ground meat. This is usually served with pita pizza.

18 OUNCES (500 G) LAMB OR BEEF
ABOUT 4 CUPS (1 L) CHOPPED PARSLEY
2 ONIONS, FINELY CHOPPED
SALT AND PEPPER

1. Mix ground beef, parsley, onions, salt, and pepper. Chop or mix everything one more time, and mix again.

2. Shape the minced mixture into an oblong roll and pinch it around the skewer. Grill over high heat until the meat is cooked through.

3. Alternate placing pieces of lamb and chicken on the skewer (such as shish taouk on the previous page).

4. Serve with pita pizza (see page 52).

كفتة الكبّاب

شيش كباب بالكفتة

٤-٦ حصص

يجب أن نقوم بالشويّ على حرارة عالية قدر الإمكان حتى يصبح الجانب الخارجي من اللحم مشوياً بشكل جيد فيحصر عصير اللحم ذو المذاق اللذيذ في الداخل. بعد تناول المقبلات (المازات) يتم عادة تناول الشيش كباب بمختلف أنواع للحوم مثل الكفتة أي (اللحم المفروم). ويقدم معه الخبز اللبناني المخصص لذلك .

٥٠٠ غم لحم خروف أو لحم الضأن المفروم
١ (ليتر) من البقدونس المفروم
٢ بصلتين مفرومتين بشكل ناعم
الملح والفلفل حسب الذوق

١- إخلط اللحم المفروم، البقدونس الفروم والبصل الفروم مع الملح والفلفل. أفرم أو إخلط كافة المحتويات مع بعضها مرة اضافية وأخلطها مرة ثانية.

٢- أجعل اللحم المفروم على شكل لفافة (أسطوانة) طويلة وثبتها على سيخ الشوي. أشويها على درجة حرارة عالية حتى ينضج اللحم بشكل كامل.

٣- نوّع الشيش كفتة مع قطع من لحم الخروف ولحم الدجاج على سبيل المثال (شيش طاووق في الصفحة السابقة).

٤- تُقدّم مع الخبز اللبناني المخصص لذلك،

Leg of Lamb the Lebanese Way

6–8 PORTIONS

This is one of Lebanon's national dishes. During festive occasions, an entire lamb is cooked the same way, but that can be difficult to do at home.

1 LAMB SHANK WITH BONE, ABOUT 2.2 POUNDS (1 KG)
6 TABLESPOONS VEGETABLE OIL
ABOUT 10½ CUPS (2½ L) OF WATER
2 CARROTS, CUT INTO PIECES
2 STALKS CELERY, CUT INTO PIECES
1 LEEK, CUT INTO PIECES
5 WHOLE CLOVES
1 WHOLE ONION
3 TABLESPOONS FINELY CHOPPED YELLOW ONION
2 TEASPOONS MINCED GARLIC
14 OUNCES (400 G) FINELY GROUND BEEF
3⅕ CUPS (700 G) LONG-GRAIN RICE, RINSED AND DRAINED
SALT
A PINCH EACH OF GROUND CARDAMOM, NUTMEG, CINNAMON, AND
   CUMIN
2 TABLESPOONS BLANCHED, PEELED ALMONDS
3 TABLESPOONS PINE NUTS
3 TABLESPOONS BUTTER
3 TABLESPOONS FLOUR
3 TABLESPOONS PISTACHIOS

1. Rub the lamb shanks with half of the oil, and roast in the oven at 400°F (200°C), until they have a nice color.

2. Boil the meat in the water in a large pot once it has gotten a nice color on all sides. Occasionally, skim the surface. Add the carrots, celery, and leek. Stick whole cloves into a whole, peeled onion, and put it in the pot. Simmer until the lamb is tender, 1 to 2 hours. Save the broth.

3. Heat the remaining oil in another pan. Add the onion and garlic. Pour into the ground meat once the onion is golden brown.

4. Lightly brown the meat, then add the rice and stir for 5 minutes. Add the spices.

5. Pour the lamb broth into the pot so that it covers the rice and a little bit more. For added color, you can add some browned onions (see the recipe for *siyyadiyyeh* on page 102).

6. Bring to a boil, cover with a lid, and simmer over low heat, or in the oven at 350°F (175°C) until the rice is cooked.

7. Cut the almonds in half lengthwise and fry them together with pine nuts, until golden brown.

8. Give it a thick consistency by melting the butter and stirring in the flour. Add a little bit of the remaining broth, little by little, while stirring continuously, until the sauce has a nice consistency. Add salt and pepper.

9. Place the rice on a platter. Add the legs of lamb shank on top, whole or cut into slices. Garnish with almonds, pine nuts, and pistachios. Serve with a salad and the sauce on the side.

خروف محشي على الطريقة اللبنانية

عدد الحصص: ١٠-٨

إلى جانب وصفة «القوزي»، المستحيل تحضيرها في البيت، إلا إذا استعملنا «قرقوراً» صغيراً، وذلك لصغر الفرن، تحضّر وصفة مشابهة ومرتكزة على استعمال فخذ الخروف فقط. وتعتبر هذه الوصفة، اليوم، من الوصفات الوطنية.

لحمة خروف من الفخذ ١ كيلو
أرز منقى، مغسول ومنقوع ٤ أكواب
زيت نباتي ٦ ملاعق كبيرة
لحم مفروم ناعم ٢ كوب
بصل مفروم ناعم ٣ ملاعق كبيرة
ثوم مدقوق ٢ ملعقة صغيرة
ملح حسب الرغبة
حب الهال، وجوزة الطيب رشة من كل صنف
قرفة وكمون رشة من كل صنف
مرقة عظام البقر ١٠ أكواب
لوز ٢ ملعقة صغيرة
زبدة ٣ ملاعق كبيرة
طحين ٣ ملاعق كبيرة
صنوبر وفستق ٣ ملاعق كبيرة من كل صنف

١- نستعمل في هذه الوصفة الفخذ. ولنا الخيار في التقديم بين أن نقطعه إلى قطع صغيرة، أو نتركه على شكله ونقدمه على وجه الأرز ونقطعه أمام الضيف.

٢- تحمّر القطع في فرن متوسط الحرارة مع القليل من الزيت.

٣- عندما تتلوّن من جميع الجهات نصفيها من الزيت والمواد الدسمة التي خرجت منها، ونسلقها في ماء يغلي. عندما تظهر الأوساخ على سطح الماء نزيلها ثم نضيف المواد المعطرة كالجزر والكراث والكرفس والبصل المشكوك بكبش القرنفل.

٤- وفيما اللحمة على النار، نضع نصف كمية الزيت الباقية في طنجرة على النار، وعندما يحمى نضيف إليه البصل المفروم فرماً ناعماً والثوم المدقوق ثم اللحم المفروم الناعم.

٥- يحرك اللحم المفروم مع القلية وعندما يصل إلى نصف النضوج نضيف إليه الأرز المصفى من ماء نقعه ونقلّب المواد معاً لمدّة خمس دقائق على النار ثم تضاف البهارات.

٦- يغمر الأرز بمرقة العظام الساخنة حتى تعلو المرقة بمعدّل ٢ سنتم. ونستطيع استعمال البصل المحروق لتلوين المرقة وبالتالي الأرز.

٧- تترك طنجرة الأرز مكشوفة، وعندما تبدأ المرقة بالغليان نغطيها وندخلها الفرن المتوسط الحرارة حتى ينضج الأرز أي يشرب المرقة، أو نتركه على موقد الغاز ولكن نخفف النار حتى الحدّ الأدنى لئلا تتبخر المرقة ويبقى الأرز غير ناضج.

٨- نسلق اللوز والفستق ثم نقشرهما، ونقطع حب اللوز إلى نصفين بجهة الطول، وبباقي الزيت نقليه مع الصنوبر حتى يشقر لونه. لا نقلي الفستق لئلا نخسر لونه الأخضر الفاتح الذي نحتاجه طالما هو اللون الأخضر الوحيد.

٩- نصنع «الرو» الأسمر من الطحين والزبدة في وعاء على النار، ونضيف إليهما باقي المرقة ونحرّك في البدء بملعقة الخشب ثم بالشريط حتى يذوب «الرو» وتشتد الصلصة ونضيف البهارات.

١٠- يسكب الأرز في إناء طويل أو مستدير ونضع قطع اللحم عليه ونزيّنه بالقلوبات. أما الصلصة فتقدّم مستقلة. ونستطيع تقديم السلطة العربية، أي مجموعة من خضر الموسم كالبندورة والخيار والخس مثلاً إلى جانب الطبق.

١١- يجب أن يكون الشكل النهائي للأرز ضارباً إلى السمرة ورطباً قليلا.

Al Torchana

IRAQI LAMB STEW WITH APRICOTS

4–6 PORTIONS

Apricots are plentiful in Iraq, so naturally they are featured often in Iraqi cuisine. Ghee is a type of clarified butter that can withstand very high temperatures and lasts for a long time. Therefore, it is common in warm Arab countries.

17.5 OUNCES (500 G) BONELESS LAMB, SUCH AS BREAST OF LAMB
2 TABLESPOONS GHEE (YOU CAN REPLACE IT WITH BUTTER OR OIL)
1 CUP (119 G) DRIED APRICOTS
⅔ CUP (80 G) SUGAR
⅓ CUP (43 G) BLANCHED ALMONDS
⅓ CUP (58 G) RAISINS, PREFERABLY YELLOW

1. Cut the meat into cubes and fry it with the *ghee* in a pan until it has a nice brown color on all sides.

2. Wash the apricots and add them into the pot. Fry for a few minutes, while continuously stirring. Then add enough water to cover the meat. Cover with a lid, and simmer until the meat is tender.

3. Add the sugar.

4. Roast the almonds in a dry frying pan until they have a nice color and add in raisins. Stir and pour the mixture into the stew.

5. Simmer until the meat is very tender. Serve with rice.

الطرشانة

المقادير:٤-٦

كوب مشمش جاف (منقوع)
١/٢ كيلو لحم غنم
١/٢ كوب لوز
١/٢ كوب زبيب
٢ ملعقة أكل دهن

١- يقطع اللحم إلى مكعبات متوسطة ومتشابهة الحجم ويغسل ويحمّر في الدهن جيدًا.

٢- يغسل المشمش الجاف ويقلب مع اللحم عدة دقائق ثم يضاف الماء بحيث يغمره ويترك ليغلي حتى ينضج اللحم.

٣- يضاف السكر.

٤- يقلى اللوز حتى يحمّر ثم يضاف معه الزبيب ويقلب قليلاً ثم يزاد إلى الوصفة.

٥- تترك على النار لمدة كافية حتى تنضج وتقدم مع الأرز المفلفل.

Couscous from Morocco

6 SERVINGS

This North African dish is very popular in Europe and the United States. The Arab world has added some of their own ingredients and flavors.

3 TABLESPOONS OLIVE OIL
1 YELLOW ONION, CUT INTO WEDGES
2 TEASPOONS GRATED GARLIC
2 CUPS (ABOUT 270 G) ZUCCHINI, CUT INTO CUBES OR CHUNKS
2 CUPS (ABOUT 270 G) EGGPLANT, CUT INTO CUBES OR CHUNKS
1 CUP GREEN BELL PEPPER (ABOUT 130 G), CUT INTO CUBES OR CHUNKS
2–3 CHICKEN BREASTS OR 1 WHOLE CHICKEN, CUT UP INTO PIECES
SALT
3 TABLESPOONS TOMATO PASTE
6⅓ CUP (1½ L) BEEF BROTH
ABOUT 1 CUP (ABOUT 200 G) COOKED CHICKPEAS
2–3 TABLESPOONS CUMIN
5¾ CUPS (1 KG) COUSCOUS
WATER
3 TABLESPOONS BUTTER
HOT SAUCE, LIKE TABASCO

1. Heat two tablespoons of oil in a large pot. First, add the onion, and after a few minutes add the garlic.

2. Add the remaining vegetables a few minutes later. Fry while stirring, until they begin to change color.

3. Cut the chicken into pieces, lightly salt it, and fry in batches until it gets a nice color. Reduce to low heat, cover with a lid, and simmer for 10 minutes. Stir occasionally.

4. Mix the tomato paste in the beef broth and pour into the pan. Add chickpeas and cumin.

5. Simmer on low heat for 30 minutes.

6. Meanwhile, put the couscous in a large heat-resistant bowl. Add a tablespoon of oil and stir. Pour boiling hot water over the couscous until it is covered and a few additional inches. Cover with a lid and set aside.

7. When the couscous has absorbed the liquid and swelled, add the butter and stir until it has dissolved.

8. Serve the couscous with the chicken and vegetables, together with a bottle of hot sauce on the side. You can also serve *merguez* (lamb sausage) and lamb chops with this couscous (as shown in the photo) if you want a real feast.

كسكس مغربي

		الوحدات الحرارية:
حُرَيْرَة	٥٧٠	
أشخاص	٦	الكمية:
دقيقة	٦٠	الوقت:

المكونات

زيت نباتي ٣ ملاعق كبيرة
بصل مقطّع إلى جوانح ٣ ملاعق كبيرة
ثوم مدقوق ٢ ملعقة صغيرة
كوسى مقطّع إلى مكعبات ٢ كوب
باذنجان مقطّع إلى مكعبات ٢ كوب
فليفلة مقطّعة إلى مكعبات ١ كوب
حمص حب مسلوق ١ كوب
دجاج مسحب ومقطّع ١ فروج
مرقة عظام البقر ٦ أكواب
زبدة ٣ ملاعق كبيرة
رب البندورة ٣ ملاعق كبيرة
كمون ٣ ملاعق كبيرة
ملح حسب الرغبة
صلصة حرة ٣ ملاعق كبيرة
كوسكوس ١ كغ

١- اشتهرت هذه الوصفة الشمال – إفريقيّة في أوروبا خاصة، وقد أُدخلت عليها النكهات العربية والمواد الجديدة في بلاد الغرب.

٢- نضع الزيت في طنجرة على النار، وعندما يحمى نضيف إليه البصل ثم الثوم.

٣- بعد بضع دقائق تضاف مكعبات الخضر المختلفة وتحرّك جيداً حتى يبدأ لونها بالتغير.

٤- تضاف عندئذ مكعّبات الدجاج واللحمة وتحرّك مع القليل من الملح حتى تتلوّن بدورها، فتغطى الطنجرة وتترك لمدة عشر دقائق مع التحريك بين الحين والآخر.

٥- بعد ذلك نضيف الحمص المسلوق والكمون والمرقة التي ذوّبنا فيها ربّ البندورة.

٦- نخفّف النار ونترك الوعاء لمدة نصف ساعة أو حتى تنضج المواد.

٧- في هذا الوقت نضع كمية ماء على النار تعادل كمية الكوسكوس المستعملة، وعندما يبدأ بالغليان نضع فيه ملعقة زيت ثم الكوسكوس الحب، ونطفيء النار ونحرك بشوكة لئلا تلتصق حبوب الكوسكوس بعضها بالبعض الآخر.

٨- عندما نرى أن الحبوب شربت الماء كله وقد كبر حجمها جراء ذلك، نضيف الزبدة ونحرّك مجدداً لتذوب وتتوزّع على جميع الحبوب.

٩- تقدم يخنة الخضر مع الكوسكوس وإلى جانبها الصلصة الحرّة المدعوة هريسة في شمال إفريقية، وهناك من يقدم أيضاً الزبيب المنقوع بالماء. كما تقدم أحياناً مع الكوسكوس تشكيلة أكبر من اللحوم كالكستليته والميرغيز، وهي هوت دوغ بلحم البقر مع البهارات الحرة، أي قريبة قليلاً من السجق الأرمنية.

Sauce for Grilled Fish

BEIRUT STYLE

4–6 PORTIONS

1 CUP (150 G) SLICED YELLOW ONIONS
1 CUP (237 ML) OLIVE OIL
5 GREEN PEPPERS, SHREDDED
3 TOMATOES
2 GREEN CHILIS, FINELY SHREDDED
2 TABLESPOONS TOMATO PASTE
3–4¼ CUPS (710–1,000 ML) OF WATER OR FISH BROTH

1. Fry the onion in oil until it is soft and translucent.

2. Add the green peppers and stir. You can also use red or yellow peppers.

3. Cut a cross in the tomatoes, scald them for 1 minute, pull away the peel, dice the flesh, and pour it into the vegetable mixture.

4. Add the chili and tomato paste, and stir for a few minutes. Then cover with water or fish broth. Simmer until the vegetables are tender.

5. Serve the sauce with grilled fish.

TRIPOLI STYLE

4–6 PORTIONS

⅖ CUP (95 ML) OLIVE OIL
2 TABLESPOONS MINCED GARLIC
1 CUP (30 G) CHOPPED FRESH CORIANDER
1 CUP (250 G) TAHINI
⅖ CUP (95 ML) LEMON JUICE
⅖ CUP (95 ML) COLD WATER

1. Heat the oil and garlic in a saucepan.

2. Add the chopped coriander when everything is hot.

3. Whisk the tahini with the lemon juice and cold water. You can also use orange juice or fish broth.

4. Pour the mixture into the saucepan. Remove the pan from the heat when the sauce begins to divide itself. Pour it over the fish.

5. You can also pour the sauce over raw fish fillets and bake them in the oven.

السمكة الحرّة

بالصلصة البيروتية

عدد الحصص: من ٦-٨ إذا قدّم كمقبلات
من ٤-٦ إذا قدّم كطبق رئيسي

لقَز رملي فرخ ٣ كيلو
زيت زيتون ١ كوب
بصل مقطع جوانح ١ كوب
فليفلة خضراء ٥ حبات
فليفلة حرّة ٢ قرن
بندورة ٥ حبات
ربّ البندورة ٢ ملعقة كبيرة

١- نضع الزيت في وعاء على النار وعندما يحمى نضيف إليه البصل المقطع إلى جوانح.

٢- حين يذبل البصل نضيف إليه الفليفلة الحلوة بعد أن نكون قد قطعناها إلى شرحات رفيعة ومن الممكن أن نشكل بالألوان مثل استعمال الفليفلة الخضراء والحمراء والصفراء مثلاً.

٣- بعد التحريك نضيف مكعبات البندورة ومن الأفضل أن نكون قد سلقناها قليلاً، مسبقا، كي نستطيع تقشيرها، فالجلدة إذا بقيت تطفو على وجه الصلصة فيما بعد وهذا شيء غير مستحب.

٤- نضيف الفليفلة الحرّة المقطعة إلى شرحات صغيرة، ثم نغمرها إما بماء معدنية أو بمرقة السمك المستخرجة من غلي خفيف لحسك السمك، وتترك الصلصة على النار حتى النضوج التام.

٥- تقدّم بالقرب من السمكة المشوية.

ملاحظة: هنالك طريقة أخرى لتحضير هذه الوصفة وذلك بوضع فيليه السمك النيّئ في صينية ستدخل الفرن ثم غمرها بالصلصة التي نكون قد حضرناها، فينضج السمك بالصلصة فيحدث تبادل جيد بالنكهات ما بين المواد.

السمكة الحرّة

بالصلصة الطرابلسية

عدد الحصص: الصلصة تكفي لـ ٣ كيلوغرامات من السمك

زيت زيتون ١/٢ كوب
ثوم مدقوق ٢ ملعقة كبيرة
كزبرة خضراء مفرومة ١ كوب
طحينة ١ كوب
عصير الحامض ١/٢ كوب
ماء بارد ١/٢ كوب

١- نضع الزيت في وعاء على النار مباشرة مع الثوم.

٢- عندما يحمى المزيج، نضيف الكزبرة ونحرك المواد بعضها ببعض.

٣- نخلط بهذا الوقت الطحينة مع عصير الحامض والماء البارد. وهنالك مَن يستعمل بدلاً عصير الأبو صفير، والقليل من مرقة السمك الناتجة عن الغليان الخفيف لحسك السمك.

٤- نضيف مزيج الطحينة إلى الثوم والكزبرة، وحين يظهر زيت الطحينة على وجه الصلصة، نطفئ النار وتقدّم بالقرب من السمكة المشوية.

Tangy Chicken with Sumac and Walnuts

8 SERVINGS

This chicken dish is absolutely delectable with a refreshing sour flavor. The original recipe contained twice the amount of garlic, but we reduced the amount a little bit. Adjust it according to your own preference.

4–6 CLOVES OF GARLIC, GRATED
2½ CUPS (593 ML) OLIVE OIL
1 CUP (237 ML) LEMON JUICE
3 LARGE LIBA OR PITA BREADS
BUTTER FOR THE DISH
SALT
2 WHOLE CHICKENS, EACH CUT INTO 8 PIECES
ALMOST 2 CUPS (ABOUT 300 G) SLICED YELLOW ONIONS
4 CUPS (125 G) CHOPPED CORIANDER LEAVES
3 TABLESPOONS WALNUTS
3 TABLESPOONS SUMAC

1. Whisk together garlic, olive oil, and lemon juice for a marinade.

2. Cut half of the pita breads into pieces, and use them to cover the bottom of a greased ovenproof dish.

3. Salt the chicken pieces and spread them and the onions on top of the bread layer.

4. Mix coriander, walnuts, and sumac with the marinade and pour it over the chicken.

5. Cover the chicken with the remaining bread, and bake at 450°F (225°C), until the chicken is cooked, about 40 minutes. If the bread gets too much color, you can cover the dish with aluminum foil.

6. Serve warm.

دجاج بمذاق حامض بالسمّاق والجوز

عدد الحصص: ٨

دجاجتان، ١٦ قطعة
كل دجاجة مقسمة إلى ٨ قطع
خبز لبناني ٣ أرغفة
بصل مقطع جوانح ٢ كوب
ثوم مدقوق ١ كوب
زيت زيتون ٢ ١/٢ كوب
عصير حامض طبيعي ١ كوب
كزبرة خضراء مفرومة ناعمة ٤ أكواب
جوز، حبّ ٣ ملاعق كبيرة
سمّاق مطحون ناعم ٣ ملاعق كبيرة
ملح حسب الرغبة

١- يخفق الثوم مع الزيت، وعصير الحامض، حتى نحصل على صلصة.

٢- نقطع الخبز إلى قطع متوسطة الحجم، ونوزّع نصفها في كعب صينية الخبيز.

٣- نوزّع، فوق الخبز، قطع الدجاج والبصل، ونرش عليها الملح.

٤- نخلط الكزبرة، والجوز، والسماق، مع الصلصة، ونوزّعها على الدجاج.

٥- نغطي الدجاج بما تبقى من خبز، وندخل الصينية فرناً حامياً حتى ينضج الدجاج. وعندما تحمرّ طبقة الخبز العليا، نضع غطاء على الصينية.

٦- يقدّم الطبق وقد جهز.

Kushari

VEGETARIAN DISH FROM EGYPT

10–15 PORTIONS

This is a very common dish in Egypt that is both satisfying and easy to prepare. In the past, this was the poor man's dish, but today you can find kushari everywhere.

1½ CUPS (355 ML) OLIVE OIL
5¼ CUPS (200 G) MACARONI, OR OTHER SMALL PASTA
2½ CUPS (475 G) RICE
3⅗ CUPS (ABOUT 760 G) COOKED CHICKPEAS, OR LENTILS
   (PLUS 1½ LITERS OF COOKING WATER OR VEGETABLE STOCK)
1 HEAPING TABLESPOON CUMIN
1 HEAPING TABLESPOON CARAWAY
1 HEAPING TABLESPOON GROUND CORIANDER
6 BLANCHED AND PEELED TOMATOES, OR 1 CAN OF WHOLE
   TOMATOES
⅔ CUP (100 G) TOMATO PASTE
1½ CUPS (225 G) SLICED YELLOW ONIONS
⅓ CUP (ABOUT 75 G) CHOPPED GARLIC

1. Heat half of the olive oil and add the pasta.

2. Stir until the pasta becomes white, then add the rinsed and drained rice. Mix well and cook for a minute.

3. Add the chickpeas or lentils, spices, and tomatoes. Mix the water from the chickpeas or lentils (or vegetable stock) with tomato paste and pour into the rice/noodle mix. Simmer over medium heat.

4. Meanwhile, heat the remaining olive oil, and fry the onion and garlic until the onions become pale golden and shiny.

5. Remove the onion and place it in a saucepan with the remaining ingredients.

6. Simmer until the pasta and rice are cooked. Serve immediately. Garnish with mint leaves and some fresh vegetables.

الكشري

عدس مسلوق ٤ أكواب
معكرونة ٢٠٠ غرام
أرز مصري كوبان ونصف
بندورة مسلوقة ومقشرة ٦ حبات
بصل جوانح كوب ونصف
ثوم مقطع ١/٤ كوب
كمون، كراوية، كزبراء جافة ملعقة كبيرة من كل نوع
زيت زيتون كوب ونصف
ماء سلق العدس ٦ أكواب
ربّ البندورة ١/٢ كوب

١- نضع نصف كوب من زيت الزيتون في وعاء على النار وأول ما يحمى نضيف إليه المعكرونة ونكون قد كسرناها إلى قطع صغيرة وكان بالإمكان إستعمال الشعيرية ولكنني ارتأيت أن المعكرونة تعطي منظرًا أجملًا للكشري.

٢- نقلب المعكرونة حتى تبدأ بالابيضاض فنضيف إليها الأرز المنقى والمغسل والمنقوع والمصفى ونقلب المواد مع بعضها البعض حتى تختلط جيدًا وتحمى.

٣- عندما يبدأ الأرز بالإلتصاق بكعب الوعاء نضيف العدس ونحرك ثم البهارات والبندورة التي نكون قد قطعناها إلى مكعبات صغيرة.

٤- نذوب ربّ البندورة بماء سلق العدس ونغمر بها المواد ونتركها على نار متوسطة.

٥- نضع بهذه الأثناء ما تبقى من زيت زيتون في مقلاة على النار وأول ما يحمى نضيف إليه البصل الجوانح والثوم المقطع وتقلب حتى يميل لون البصل إلى الأصفر الباهت المشقر فنصفيه من زيته ونضيف هذه القلية إلى الكشري على النار.

٦- تترك الوصفة حتى الإستواء الكامل للأرز والمعكرونة ثم تقدم مباشرة.

Siyyadiyyeh

BAKED FISH WITH SPICY RICE

6–8 PORTIONS

A specialty in coastal cities such as Tripoli, Byblos, Sidon, and Tyre. The name may derive from Sidon, but personally I think that this dish has its roots in Beirut.

5½–6½ POUNDS (2½–3 KG) WHOLE WHITE FISH SUCH AS SEA
    BASS, COD, OR WALLEYE
ANY CARROTS, ONIONS, AND LEEKS FOR THE BROTH
SALT
6 CUPS (900 G) SLICED YELLOW ONIONS
3⅘ CUPS (900 ML) VEGETABLE OIL
1 CUP (135 G) PINE NUTS
1 CUP (140 G) BLANCHED AND PEELED ALMONDS
5 TABLESPOONS BUTTER
3 CUPS (555 G) LONG-GRAIN RICE
1 TABLESPOON CUMIN
1 TABLESPOON CINNAMON
1 TABLESPOON CARAWAY
1 TEASPOON GROUND CORIANDER
3 TABLESPOONS FLOUR
2 LEMONS

1. Clean and fillet the fish. Set the fillets aside.

2. Place the fish bones and heads in a saucepan with cold water and bring to a boil.

3. Simmer for 1 hour and skim the surface a few times. You can also add pieces of carrots, onions, and leek to add flavor to the broth.

4. Strain the broth, add salt, and set aside.

5. Place the fish fillets in an ovenproof dish and cover with 2 cups of the fish broth. Bake at 350°F (175°C) until the fish is cooked, about 15 to 20 minutes. Cover and set aside.

6. Fry the sliced onion in about ⅘ cup of oil, while stirring continuously, until it is golden brown. Lift out a third of the onion. Continue to fry the rest until it gets a dark brown color. Drain the onion and save the oil. Add the dark brown onion to the broth and cook for a few minutes.

7. Fry the pine nuts and almonds (save some for garnish) golden brown in the same oil that the onions were fried in. Add two tablespoons of butter and the remaining oil.

8. Add the rice when the butter has melted and the oil is hot. Stir, and ensure that all the grains are shiny from the fat.

9. Add the spices while stirring.

10. Strain the broth to get rid of the browned onion. It is only used to give the broth some color.

11. Pour enough broth over the rice to cover it. Cover with a lid and cook on low heat, or in the oven at 350°F (175°C).

12. Melt the remaining butter. Add flour and stir until it becomes brown (*en roux*). Pour the rest of the stock into the butter and stir until the flour is completely dissolved. Add ⅖ cup of lemon juice.

13. Place the cooked rice on a serving plate. Place the fish fillets on top. Garnish with pine nuts, almonds, the golden brown onions, and lemon wedges. Serve with sauce on the side, and if you want, a little bit of toasted liba bread.

الصيادية

عدد الحصص: ٦-٨

الصيادية وصفة ساحلية نجدها في المدن الساحلية الرئيسية كطرابلس وجبيل والبترون وصيدا وصور.

ومن الممكن أن تكون كلمة صيادية تحريفاً لكلمة صيداوية. ولكني أعتقد أنه من بيروت انطلقت هذه الوصفة إلى لبنان، نظراً لصعوبة تنفيذها ودقّة مراحلها. فبيروت بفنادقها وحياتها الفندقية المطبخية المتطوّرة نسبة لباقي المدن الساحلية، أفضل مرشحة لتكون نقطة إنطلاقها.

سمك اللقّز الرملي الكامل ٣ كيلو
بصل مقطّع جوانح ٦ أكواب
زيت نباتي ٤ أكواب
أرزّ أصفر حبّ طويل ٣ أكواب
عصير حامض ١/٢ كوب
كمون، قرفة، كراوية ١ ملعقة كبيرة من كل صنف
كزبراء يابسة ناعمة ١ ملعقة صغيرة
صنوبر، لوز مسلوق ومقشّر ١ كوب من كلّ صنف
طحين ٣ ملاعق كبيرة
زبدة ٥ ملاعق كبيرة
ملح حسب الرغبة
حامض ٢ حبة

١- تمتاز الصيادية بثلاثة عناصر مهمّة: نوعية السمك، المرق المستخرج من عظام السمك، والصلصة المُرافقة.

٢- أفضل سمك يُستعمل للصيادية هو ما يُسمى باللقّز، وأظن أنه من الأسماك التي تكثر في الشاطئ اللبناني قديما، أما اليوم فأصبح من النادر اصطياده، فأدخل الاستيراد مكانه أسماكاً شبيهة له، أكان من السنغال أو من مصر أو من تركيا. وبالعموم نستطيع استعمال أي سمك بحري مستدير أبيض اللون، على أن يكون طازجا.

٣- يُنظف السمك جيداً وتسحب الفيليه من العظم والرأس وتحفظ جانبا.

٤- نضع العظم والرأس في وعاء على النار ونغمرها بالماء البارد، وعندما تصل إلى درجة الغليان نلاحظ ظهور رغوة صفراء اللون على سطح الماء، فنزيلها ثم نخفّف النار بشكل يبقى معه السطح مرتعشاً.

٥- نترك الوعاء على النار لمدة الساعة، ومن الممكن إضافة الجزر والبصل والكرات إليه للتطييب.

٦- بعد مرور الساعة نطفئ تحت الوعاء ونصفيه، فنحصل هكذا على المرق التي هي أساس وصفتنا.

٧- نضع الفيليه في الصينية ونوزّع عليها كوبان من المرق وندخلها فرناً متوسط الحرارة وذلك حتى تنضج، فنخرجها من الفرن ونضع عليها غطاء ونحفظها جانباً.

٨- نضع كوب من الزيت النباتي على النار وحين يحمى نضيف إليه البصل المقطع إلى جوانح ونباشر بالتحريك بين الحين والآخر حتى يُصبح لون البصل ذهبياً مثل «جوانح الدبور» فنأخذ منه ثلث الكمية ونحفظه جانبا، أما الكمية المتبقية في الزيت فنتركها على النار حتى يصبح لونها كاحلا، عندها نصفيها من الزيت ونضعها في المرق ونتركها تغلي معه قليلا.

٩- أما الزيت الذي لونا به البصل فنرجعه إلى المقلاة، ونستفيد منه ما دام حامياً لتلوين الصنوبر واللوز تلويناً ذهبيا.

١٠- نضع ما تبقّى من الزيت النباتي مع ملعقتين كبيرتين من الزبدة، على النار في الوعاء.

١١- عندما يذوب المزيج ويحمى، نضيف الأرز، ونباشر بالتحريك حتى تغلّف المواد الدهنية كل حبّة أرز.

١٢- نضيف عند ذلك البهارات، ونحرّك كي تتوزّع جيداً.

١٣- عندما نرى أنّ الأرز قد وصل إلى خطر الالتصاق في قعر الوعاء، نضيف مرق السمك، لكن من خلال مصفاة لالتقاط جوانح البصل السوداء التي استعملناها لتلوينه.

١٤- يُغمر الأرزّ بالمرق، وحين يبدأ السطح بالغليان، نخفف النار ونضع غطاءً على الوعاء ونتركه حتى ينضج، ويمكن أيضاً أن نضعه داخل فرن متوسط الحرارة.

١٥- نذوب، في هذه الأثناء، ما تبقّى من الزبدة في وعاء على النار، ونضيف إليها الطحين، ونباشر بالتحريك حتى نحصل على عجينة سمراء اللون، نضيف إليها ما تبقّى من المرق، أو ما يعادل الأربعة أكواب، ونعاود التحريك حتى تذوب العجينة السمراء كلياً داخل المرق، فيشتدّ هذا الأخير، وهكذا نحصل على الصلصة، ونختم تحضيرها بإضافة نصف كوب من عصير الحامض عليها.

١٦- عندما تنضح حبات الأرز، تسكب في وعاء التقديم، وتوزّع عليها فيليه السمك، ويُزيّن الطبق بالقلوبات وجوانح البصل وشرحات الحامض، وتقدم الصلصة بقربه.

١٧- هذه هي الطريقة المفضلة لديّ لتحضير الصيادية، فهي تحفظ شكل السمك الجميل مما يسمح لنا بتقديم طبق جميل المظهر وشهي.

ملاحظة: وهنالك طريقة أخرى لتحضير الصيادية، تكون بتقطيع السمك إلى شرحات بالعرض وقليها بجلدها بزيت الزيتون حتى تتلوّن، ومن ثم وضعها بالماء على النار، وتركها حتى تنضج، ومن ثم ترفع عن النار، وتُسحب الفيليه من العظم. أما المرق فيستعمل لتحضير الأرز والصلصة، مع الاستعانة بالبصل المحروق لإعطاء اللون للأرز. وهنالك مَن يستعمل السكر المحروق لهذا الغرض، ولكن هذا طبعاً ممنوع، ومخالف لقواعد الطبخ، إذ يدخل مكوّن على الوصفة لا علم للمستهلك به.

هاتان الوصفتان شبيهتان إلا في طريقة طهي السمك وتقديمه. ففي الأولى احتراف إذ يُظهر الطاهي مهارته في تسحيب الفيليه كاملة من العظم، وتحفظ أيضاً شكل السمك عند التقديم.

Turkey the Lebanese Way with Chestnuts

10–15 PORTIONS

A relatively new dish in Lebanon, which is now served during Christmas and New Year. When I cooked it on TV, it became a huge success.

2 TABLESPOONS FINELY CHOPPED YELLOW ONION
4 TABLESPOONS MINCED GARLIC
4 TABLESPOONS BUTTER
8 OUNCES (225 G) GROUND BEEF
6 CUPS (1.1 KG) LONG-GRAIN RICE
SALT, PEPPER, CUMIN, CARDAMOM, NUTMEG, AND
  (OPTIONAL) MASTIC

1 TURKEY, ABOUT 9 POUNDS (4 KG)
10½ CUPS (2½ L) CHICKEN BROTH
ABOUT 1½ CUPS (225 G) CHESTNUTS
INTESTINES FROM THE TURKEY
SALT
3 TABLESPOONS ROASTED PINE NUTS
3 TABLESPOONS ROASTED, BLANCHED, AND PEELED ALMONDS
3 TABLESPOONS PISTACHIOS

1. Fry the onions and half of the garlic in a saucepan with 2 tablespoons of butter. Add the ground meat and brown it.

2. Rinse the rice and allow it to drain thoroughly and pour it into the ground meat, together with the spices. Mix well.

3. Sauté for about 5 minutes, then use about 2 cups of the rice mixture to fill the turkey. Make sure the bird is properly thawed if it has been frozen.

4. Place the stuffed turkey in a greased roasting pan and roast in the oven at 350°F (175°C). Baste the turkey a few times with the gravy and a little bit of chicken broth. Cover with foil when it is nicely browned, and let it stand until clear, about 1 to 3 hours depending on the size. The internal temperature should be around 175°F (80°C).

5. Cover the rest of the rice mixture with the remaining chicken broth. Bring to a boil, cover with a lid, and place in the oven until the rice is cooked.

6. Cut a cross in the bottom of each chestnut, and roast them in the oven at 450°F (225°C) for 25 minutes.

7. Mix the turkey intestines with the remaining garlic. Melt 2 tablespoons of butter over low heat and add the intestinal mixture. Fry for a few minutes and add a bit of gravy from the turkey. Add salt to the sauce.

8. Spread the rice mixture on a large serving dish. Place the turkey on top. Garnish with pine nuts, almonds, pistachios, and chestnuts. You can also serve the turkey with small, ovenbaked potatoes instead of rice, as pictured.

الحبش المحشو شرقي

عدد الحصص: ١٠-١٥

في الفترة الأخيرة، برزت هذه الوصفة في المطبخ اللبناني، خاصة في عشاء ليلة عيد الميلاد أو ليلة رأس السنة، حتى أصبحت الطبق الوطني لهاتين المناسبتين. وأذكر أني حين طبخت الحبش على الطريقة الغربية خلال برنامجي التلفزيوني، لاقت أيضاً نجاحاً وقبولاً، وبدأت تعتمد من قبل البعض.

يُطبخ الحبش بطريقة مشابهة للدجاج الشرقي ولكني سأعرض الآن الطريقة السهلة والعصرية.

ديك رومي (حبش) ٤٥٠٠غرام
أرز حب طويل مغسول ٦ أكواب
لحم مفروم ناعم ٢٥٠ غرام
صنوبر ٣ ملاعق
فستق مسلوق ومقشّر ٣ ملاعق كبيرة
لوز مسلوق ومقشّر ٣ ملاعق كبيرة
كستناء ٢٥٠ غرام
ثوم مدقوق ٤ ملاعق
مرقة الدجاج ١٠ أكواب
بصل مفروم ناعم ٢ ملعقة كبيرة
سمنة ١ كوب
طحالات الديك المستعمل
ملح، بهار، كمون حسب الرغبة
حبّ الهال، مستكة حسب الرغبة
جوزة الطيب حسب الرغبة

١- توضع ملعقتان كبيرتان من السمنة في طنجرة على النار، وعندما تذوب يُضاف البصل ونصف كمية الثوم، ثم اللحمة المفرومة.

٢- تحرّك اللحمة،ثم يُضاف إليها الأُرز المصفّى جيداً من ماء نقعه، ويحرّكان معاً حتى تختلط اللحمة بالأُرز، فتُضاف البهارات المذكورة.

٣- بعد مرور بضع دقائق، يستخرج كوبان من حشوة الأُرز فيُحشى بهما الديك الرومي بعدما أزيل تجميده بالطريقة الصحيحة، وتأكّدنا أنّ داخله لم يعد مجمّداً أيضاً. وأفضل طريقة لإزالة التجميد هي وضعه في أسفل البراد لئلا تتساقط ماء التجميد على باقي الموجودات، مما يؤدي إلى انتقال الجراثيم.

٤- نضع الديك في صينية داخل فرن متوسط الحرارة وفي قعرها القليل من السمنة، ونتركها حتى النضوج الكامل. ونحرص أن نسقيه بين الحين والآخَر بمرقة عظام الدجاج، كما نضع ورقة أليمنيوم على صدره عندما يحمرّ لئلا يحترق.

٥- يُغمر باقي الأُرز بكمية كافية من المرقة، وعندما تبدأ بالغليان، نضع غطاء على الطنجرة، وندخلها إلى فرن متوسط الحرارة حتى النضوج الكامل.

٦- نضع الكستناء في صينية بعد أن نقطع كعبها، وندخلها الفرن حتى تتكسّر قشرتها فيسهل تقشيرها.

٧- نضع في طنجرة على نار متوسطة الحرارة ملعقة صغيرة من السمنة. وعندما تحمى، نضيف إليها الطحالات المطحونة مع الثوم المدقوق. ثم نضيف إليهما بعد بضع دقائق بعضاً من خواص الديك المستخرج من صينية التحمير. فنحصل هكذا على الصلصة النهائية التي نعدّل نكهتها بالقليل من الملح إذا أردنا.

٨- نسكب الأُرز في جاط التقديم، ونضع الديك عليه، ونوزّع فوقهما الصنوبر، واللوز، والفستق، والكستناء. وتقدّم الصلصة منفردة بعد أن نصفّيها.

٩- أما الأُرز الموجود داخل الديك، فينضج بسبب امتصاصه الخواص السائل.

Mansaf

LEG OF LAMB FROM JORDAN

5 PORTIONS

This is the unofficial national dish of Jordan. Jameed is a kind of dried yogurt that may be purchased and dissolved in water.

1 LAMB SHANK, SPLIT INTO SMALLER PIECES
10 CARDAMOM PODS
10 WHOLE CLOVES
10 BAY LEAVES
WHITE PEPPER
1 PIECE OF JAMEED, CAN BE REPLACED WITH APPROXIMATELY
    4 CUPS (1 L) GREEK YOGURT
ABOUT 5½ CUPS (1 KG) RICE
SALT
¾ CUP (177 ML) GHEE, OR VEGETABLE OIL
WATER
0.02 OUNCE (½ G) SAFFRON
1 LIBA BREAD OR LARGE PITA BREAD
FRESHLY GROUND BLACK PEPPER
1¾ CUPS ROASTED ALMONDS (250 G)
ABOUT 1¾ CUPS (250 G) ROASTED PINE NUTS OR RAW PISTACHIOS

1. Rinse the meat, put it in a large pot, and cover with water. Skim the surface at regular intervals when the water has boiled. Continue skimming until the liquid becomes clear. Add half of the cardamom, cloves, bay leaves, and some white pepper. Simmer over medium heat until the meat is almost cooked. Remove the pot from the heat, strain, and save the broth.

2. If you get a hold of *jameed*: break it into pieces and soak in warm water overnight. Run in the blender the next day, strain, and bring to a boil. Add the lamb and the broth. Simmer over low heat until the meat is tender.

   If you are using Greek yogurt: bring to a boil while stirring continuously. Add the lamb and the broth and continue as above.

3. Meanwhile, soak the rice in warm water for 10 minutes.

   Drain. Boil in a saucepan with a little bit of salt, fat, and enough water to cover the rice. Add the remaining cardamom, bay leaves, cloves, and saffron. Boil over high heat for 5 minutes, until the rice has absorbed all the liquid. Lower the heat and continue to cook until the rice is ready.

4. Cover a large platter with liba bread or pita bread. Sprinkle with a little bit of yogurt broth. Spread rice and lamb on top. Turn the pepper mill a few times over the dish. Decorate with nuts and maybe a chili. Serve the yogurt broth in a bowl on the side.

المنسف الاردني

المقادير :

نحتاج إلى فخذ من الخروف البلدي (الاوزي) أو الغنم حسب الرغبة ونقوم بتقطيع لحمه إلى قطع بحجم نصف كف اليد.

جميد (نوع من الكشك المجفف على شكل كريات) أو كشك هكذا نسميه في الأردن كيلو من الأرز (أسباني).

رغيف من خبز التنور.

نصف كيلو من اللوز والصنوبر محمّص بسمن حموي.

عشر حبات مشكلة من الهال وكبش القرنفل.

طريقة التحضير :

تغسل اللحمة جيدًا ثم نضع غمرها ماءً ونضعها على النار وعندما تبدأ بالغليان ننزع منها الزفرة. ثم نضيف إليها حب الهال وورق الغار وكبش القرنفل وقليلاً من الفلفل الأبيض ونتركها على النار حتى النضوج وبعدها نرفعها عن النار.

قبل النوم نكون قد كسّرنا الجميد أو الكشك ونقعناه في ماء فاتر حتى اليوم الثاني.

وفي اليوم التالي نضع الجميد في الخلاط حتى يصبح اللبن الأبيض ثم نحضر منخلاً من السلك ونقوم بتصفيته من الشوائب ونضعه على النار ونقوم بتحريكه حتى يبدأ بالغليان ثم نرفع قطع اللحم ونضيفها إلى اللبن ثم نصفّي مرق اللحم بالمنخل ونضيفها إلى الجميد ونضع المجموع على نار متوسطة حتى النضوج.

في هذه الأثناء نكون قد نقعنا الأرز بماء فاتر لمدة ١٠ دقائق نصفيه ونضعه في طنجرة الطبخ ونضيف إليه ماء مغليًا مع ملح وسمن بلدي أو حموي، وحب الهال وكبش القرنفل وربع ملعقة صغيرة من الزعفران الأصفر. ونتركه على نار عالية مدة ٥ دقائق حتى يشرب الأرز الماء ثم نقوم بطهيه على نار هادئة.

من مقومات المنسف الجيّد والصحيح هو أن تكون كل حبة بحبة من الأرز.

نحضر صينية دائرية ونضع في قعرها رغيف التنور ثم نحضر قليلاً من الجميد المطبوخ ونبلل به الرغيف وبعدها نحضّر الأرز ونفرشه على الرغيف ونحضّر قطع اللحم ونصفّها فوق الأرز ونزينه بالصنوبر واللوز المحمّرين وبعدها نرش القليل من الفلفل الأسود الناعم فوق الصينية. ونقوم بوضع اللبن في وعاء عميق مع ملعقة كبيرة لكي نرش اللبن على الأرز أثناء الأكل.

Majbous

LAMB DISH FROM THE UNITED ARAB EMIRATES

6–8 PORTIONS

Vegetables are not very common in the United Arab Emirates. So instead, they often use spices such as cloves, cardamom, and saffron to add flavor to the cuisine.

2¼ POUNDS (1 KG) LAMB MEAT, WITH BONE
A BUNDLE OF FRESH HERBS
1 WHOLE ONION, PEELED
1 TABLESPOON WHOLE CLOVES
2 CUPS (473 ML) GHEE, OIL, OR BUTTER
3 CUPS (450 G) FINELY CHOPPED YELLOW ONION
⅘ CUP (160 G) CHICKPEAS, COOKED
⅘ CUP (120 G) RAISINS, SOAKED
1 TEASPOON GROUND DRIED LIMES (OR GRATED LIME PEEL)
0.02 OUNCE (½ G) SAFFRON
1 TEASPOON GROUND CARDAMOM
⅕ CUP (47 ML) ROSE AND ORANGE BLOSSOM WATER, MIXED
4 CUPS RICE, SOAKED AND RINSED
SALT
⅔ CUP (57 G) ROASTED ALMONDS

1. Put the meat in a large pot of boiling water and salt. Skim off while the water is boiling until the liquid becomes clear.

2. Add fresh herbs and a whole onion with cloves that have been put inside.

3. Simmer over medium heat until the meat is tender. Lift out the meat, strain, and save the broth.

4. Add about ⅔ cup of fat in a frying pan and allow it to melt (if you aren't using oil) over medium heat. Add the chopped onion and stir while you brown it. Add a little bit of water and keep stirring until everything has a light brown color.

5. Add a tablespoon of fat along with chickpeas, raisins, and dried lime. Stir over low heat, then turn off the heat. In the Gulf kitchen, this is called "the filling."

6. Mix the saffron and cardamom with the rose and orange blossom water and set aside.

7. Rinse the rice twice. Place it in a pot and add enough broth to cover it, plus a little bit extra. Cook over low heat until the rice is ready.

8. Meanwhile, brown the meat in the remaining fat, and set aside.

9. Place the rice on a serving plate and pour the spice mixture with the rose and orange blossom water over the rice. Spread the "filling" on top. Lastly, place the browned meat on top and garnish with almonds. Serve immediately.

مجبوس اللحم

عدد الحصص: ٦-٨
مدة التحضير بالتفصيل:
سلق اللحم: ٤٠-٦٠ دقيقة
الحشوة والأرزّ: ٤٠ دقيقة

المكونات:

لحم غنم بعظمه ١ كلغ (من الظهر)
أرزّ منقى ومغسّل ومنقوع ٤ أكواب
حمّص مسلوق ومقشر ١ كوب
زبيب منقوع بالماء ١ كوب
بصل مفروم ناعماً ٣ أكواب
باقة أعشاب معطّرة ١
بصلة كاملة ١
كبش القرنفل حبًّا ١ ملعقة كبيرة
لومي أسود ناعم ١ ملعقة صغيرة
زعفران هال ناعم ١ ملعقة صغيرة
هال ناعم ١ ملعقة صغيرة
ماء ورد وماء زهر ١/٤ كوب مختلط
لوز مقشّر ١ كوب
سمن ٢ كوبان
ملح حسب الرغبة

طريقة التحضير:

١- يغسل اللحم ويوضع في ماء يغلي وفور رجوعه إلى الغليان نلاحظ ظهور رغوة بنيّة رماديّة اللون على سطح الماء فننزلها وذلك مراراً حتى لا تعاود الظهور.

٢- نضع باقة الأعشاب المطيّبة في الماء مع البصلة الكاملة وقد وزّعنا عليها حبّات كبش القرنفل.

٣- يترك اللحم على نار متوسّطة حتى النضج التام فيرفع ويحفظ جانباً ويصفّى ماء السلق ويحفظ جانباً أيضاً.

٤- نضع كوباً من السمن في مقلاة على نار متوسّطة وما إن يذوب ويحمى حتى نضيف إليها البصل ونقلبه بين الحين والآخر ويترك حتى يشقر فنضيف إليه القليل من الماء ونقلبه مجدداً ونتركه حتى يميل لونه إلى البني الفاتح.

٥- نضيف حينها ملعقة كبيرة من السمن ثم الحمّص والزبيب المصفّى واللوز المقشّر واللومي الأسود وتقلب جميع المواد على نار هادئة ثم نطفئ النار ونتركها جانباً. وهذا ما يسمى في المطبخ الخليجي «الحشوة».

٦- نخلط الزعفران والهال الناعم في خليط ماء الورد وماء الزهر ونتركهما جانباً.

٧- نصفي الأرزّ من ماء نقعه ونغسله مجدداً ثم نضعه في ماء سلق اللحم وقد رفعناه إلى درجة الغليان. يترك الأرزّ حتى ينضج.

٨- في هذه الأثناء، نحمّر قطع اللحم المسلوقة في ما تبقى من سمن ثم نحفظها جانباً.

٩- نسكب الأرزّ المسلوق في قصعة التقديم ويوزّع عليه القليل من سمن تحمير اللحمة ثم خليط الزعفران والهال وماء الورد والزهر ثم الحشوة وتوزّع قطعة اللحم المسلوقة المحمّرة على سطح الأرزّ ويقدّم الطبق فوراً.

ملاحظة: تقدّم أحياناً مع «مجبوس اللحم» وصفة «المصقعة».

Kabsa with al-Yadam

LAMB DISH FROM SAUDI ARABIA

10 SERVINGS

Kabsa is a dish that is popular throughout the Arab world under different names and with many different variations of it. Al-Yadam is also served with chicken or fish.

10 PIECES OF MEAT FROM THE FRONT OF THE LAMB, EACH PIECE
    4.6–5.3 OUNCES (135–150 G)
2 CUPS (473 ML) OIL, OR GHEE
2 BAY LEAVES
6 CARROTS, CUT INTO PIECES
1 WHOLE YELLOW ONION
2 TABLESPOONS WHOLE CLOVES
1½ CUPS (225 G) THINLY SLICED YELLOW ONION
1 TABLESPOON GRATED GARLIC
3 CUPS (408 G) DICED EGGPLANT
3 CUPS (570 G) RICE, RINSED AND DRAINED

KABSA SPICE BLEND
1 TEASPOON EACH OF DRIED LIME, GROUND CORIANDER,
    TURMERIC, CUMIN, CINNAMON, AND GINGER

AL-YADAM
ABOUT 6 CUPS THINLY SLICED ONIONS
3 CUPS (710 ML) WATER
2 CUPS (242 G) SOAKED RAISINS
⅖ CUP (95 ML) OIL, OR GHEE
SALT

AL-YADAM SPICE MIXTURE
1 TABLESPOON EACH OF GROUND CORIANDER, CINNAMON,
    TURMERIC, CUMIN, AND GROUND CARDAMOM

1. Brown the meat in batches with a bit of fat. Place it in a roasting pan and roast it in the oven at 450°F (225°C), until it is nicely browned on all sides.

2. Transfer the meat to a large pot filled with cold water.

3. Bring to a boil, then simmer on low heat and add bay leaves, carrots, and a whole onion with cloves put inside it.

4. Check if the meat is tender after 50 minutes. If it is, take it out of the pot. Otherwise, cook it a little bit longer. Save the broth.

5. Heat the remaining oil and fry the onion and garlic while stirring. Add the eggplant and meat after a few minutes. Fry for a while.

6. Add rice and the *kabsa* spice blend. Pour enough broth to cover the rice. Bring to boil and cover with a lid. Slowly finish cooking at 400°F (200°C) until the rice is ready.

7. In the meantime, make the *al-Yadam*. Place the onion in a saucepan. Add 2 cups of water. Cook until all the water is absorbed and the onions are browned.

8. While stirring, add 1 cup water, raisins, fat, the *al-Yadam* spice mixture, and salt. Fry for a few minutes.

9. Place the food on a plate. Spread the *al-Yadam* on top.

الكبـسـة

(دجاج أو لحم أو سمك) مع اليدام الحشوة الخليجية

عدد الحصص:١٠-١٠
مدة التحضير: ساعة ونصف
سلق اللحم:٠٠ دقيقة تقريبًا
الكبسة: ٤٠ دقيقة
اليدام: ٣٠ دقيقة

المكونات:

الكبسة:

زيت (أو سمن) ٢ كوبان
بصل مفروم ناعماً كوب ونصف
ثوم مدقوق ١ ملعقة كبيرة
باذنجان مقطّع مكعّبات٢ كوبان (٤-٥ حبّات)
لحم مستخرج من الفخذ١٠ قطع (كل واحدة بوزن ١٣٥-١٥٠ غ)
باقة أعشاب معطّرة ١ (راجع وصفة امبلح السمك)
جزر ٦ حبّات
بصلة كاملة٢
كبش قرنفل حبّ ٢ ملعقتان كبيرتان
بهارات الكبسة ٣ ملاعق كبيرة
(لومي مجفف، كزبرة جافّة، قرفة ناعمة، كركم، كمّون، زنجبيل)

اليدام:

بصل مفروم ناعماً ٦ أكواب
زبيب منقوع في ماء بارد ٢ كوبان
حمّص مسلوق ومقشّر ٣ أكواب
سمن ٢/١ كوب

بهارات اليدام:

كزبرة جافّة ناعمة ١ ملعقة صغيرة
قرفة ناعمة، كركم، كمّون،
هال ناعم ١ ملعقة صغيرة من كل نوع
ملح حسب الرغبة

١ - ندهن قطع اللحم بالقليل من الزيت ونضعها في صينية وندخلها فرنًا حامٍيًا حتى تتلوّن جيداً من جميع الجهات.

٢ - نرفعها من الصينية ونضعها على نار قويّة في وعاء بداخله ماء بارد.

٣ - ما إن يبدأ الماء بالغليان حتى نلاحظ ظهور رغوة رمادية/بنيّة اللون على سطح الماء فنزيلها ونواصل إزالتها حتى لا تعاود الظهور فنضع باقة الأعشاب المعطّرة، والجزر والبصل الذي تمّ توزيع كبش القرنفل عليه.

٤ - بعد حوالي ٥٠ دقيقة نفحص درجة النضج، وإذا شعرنا بأن اللحم أصبح طريًا نرفعه من المرق الذي نصفيه ونحفظه واللحم جانباً.

٥ - نضع ما تبقى من الزيت في وعاء على النار المتوسطة وحين يحمى نضيف إليه البصل ومن ثم الثوم.

٦ - بعد التحريك لبضع دقائق نباشر بإضافة مكعّبات الباذنجان ومن ثم قطع اللحم.

٧- بعد بضع دقائق نضيف الأرزّ وبهارات الكبسة وتغمر المواد بماء سلق اللحم وحين

Desserts & Pastries

الحلويات

Closed Katayef

LEBANESE CREPES

26 PIECES

These pastries are similar to pancakes with filling. You can serve them open or closed. Ashta is reminiscent of British clotted cream, and it is a regular feature in Lebanese desserts but can be difficult to get a hold of in the United States. You can make it yourself or replace it with a simpler alternative.

6 CUPS (750 G) FLOUR
1 TABLESPOON DRY YEAST
6 CUPS (1⅖ L) MILK
ABOUT 1¾ TABLESPOONS (25 G) BUTTER

FILLING

3 CUPS (280 G) GROUND WALNUTS
1 CUP (200 G) SUGAR
1 TABLESPOON ROSE WATER
2 TABLESPOONS ORANGE BLOSSOM WATER
3 CUPS (ABOUT 680 G) ASHTA PUDDING (SEE RECIPE ON PAGE 123);
    ALTERNATIVE: COTTAGE CHEESE OR RICE PUDDING
6⅓ CUPS (1½ L) FRYING OIL
3 CUPS (700 ML) SUGAR SYRUP (SEE RECIPE ON PAGE 136)

1. Heat the milk to 125°F (50°C). Mix flour, yeast, and milk to a smooth batter. Allow to rise in a warm place until it has doubled in size.

2. Carefully pour about ⅔ of a cup of the batter onto a hot and greased baking tray on top of the stove, or in a pancake maker with a bit of butter.

3. Flip the pancake with a spatula when the underside has a nice golden color. Cook for a few more seconds. Set aside.

4. Mix walnuts, sugar, and rose and orange blossom water. Add a tablespoon of the mixture in the middle of the pancake, and repeat this process with a third of the pancakes. Add a tablespoon of *ashta* pudding on the second third of the pancakes. Save the last third for open crepes (see the following page).

5. Fold the pancakes in half around the filling and press at the edges so that they stick together. Fry in hot oil until they are golden brown. Let the pancakes drain off for a little bit. Pour some of the sugar syrup over the fried pancakes and press at the edges for another minute.

القطايف المغلقة

عدد الحصص: ٢٤ حبّة صغيرة تقريبًا

قصدت محلات رفيق الرشيدي للحصول على تفاصيل دخوله الصنعة، وكيف كانت القطايف والعشلية والقشطة تحضّر في القديم. ولكنّ وجدت ان الحاج قد توفي، فإذا بي أهتدي بمساعدة أولاده إلى السيد محمد حسّون في برج البراجنة، وكان المعلم الرئيسي عند الحاج رفيق.

إنطلاقًا من سوق الملبس ومرورا بساحة السمك، كنا نصل إلى سوق أبو النصر، حيث يوجد المحل التجاري للرشيدي. وكان سوق القطايف قديمًا مكان البرلمان الحالي. وفي غياب الغاز، كان يستعمل الدقّ ويوضع في وسطه الفحم. وعندما يجمّر، كان يوزّع على الدقّ وتوضع «شواريق» لتأجيج الحرارة تحت الصدر، فتجهز فيه الكنافة، ثم العشلية، والبورما، والبلورية، والفيصلية، والقطايف.

طحين ٦ أكواب
خميرة ١ ملعقة كبيرة
حليب سائل ٦ أكواب
قشطة طازجة ٣ أكواب
قشطة مطبوخة ٣ أكواب
جوز مجروش ٣ أكواب
سكر ناعم ١ كوب
ماء ورد ١ ملعقة كبيرة
ماء زهر ٢ ملعقة كبيرة
زهر الليمون أو مربى الورد ١/٢ كوب
فستق ناعم ١/٢ كوب
زيت للقلي ٦ أكواب
قطر ٣ أكواب

١- نخفق الطحين والخميرة مع الحليب حتى نحصل على عجينة متماسكة وطريّة ونتركها حتى يتضاعف حجمها.

٢- نملأ بكمية منها كيس سكب ذا رأس حديدي مستدير، ونبدأ بسكب دوائر صغيرة على صينية حديدية وضعناها على الموقد أو الوجاق، وإذا كان الأخير موجودا فيكون ذلك أفضل.

٣- قياس قطر الدوائر فأمر يرجع للشخص، إذ نستطيع سكب قطع قطايف صغيرة أو كبيرة، حسب الرغبة.

٤- بعد دقيقة من سكب القطع نقلب الحبات لبضع ثوان على الجهة المعاكسة بمساعدة المقشط، ثم نرفعها عن النار.

٥- نخلط الجوز المجروش مع السكر الناعم وماء الورد وماء الزهر ونوزّعها بمقدار ملعقة صغيرة في وسط عجينة القطايف.

٦- نفعل الشيء نفسه بالقشطة المطبوخة مع دوائر عجينة أخرى ونطبق العجين في الحالتين على الحشوة ونلحم الطرفين معاً بحيث تكون الحشوة في الداخل، ثم نقلي هذه الحبات بالزيت الحامي حتى تتلوّن ثم نضعها في القطر ونكبسها بالمكبس لبضع دقائق.

٧- نوزّع القشطة الطازجة على ما تبقى من عجين ونطوي العجين من جهة واحدة حتى نصف الحبة بحيث تبقى القشطة ظاهرة.

٨- نوزّع زهر الليمون على القشطة والفستق الناعم ويقدّم القطر على حدة.

Open Katayef

OPEN LEBANESE CREPES

8 SMALL PORTIONS

Serve the last third of the pancakes open with the filling visible. In Lebanon, fresh ashta, a kind of clotted cream, is usually used for the filling. You can replace it with sour cream or ricotta.

⅓ PANCAKE BATTER (SEE RECIPE PAGE 119)
3 CUPS (ABOUT 680 G) FRESH ASHTA, SEE RECIPE BELOW;
    ALTERNATIVE: COTTAGE CHEESE, SOUR CREAM, OR RICOTTA
⅔ CUP (38 G) GROUND PISTACHIOS
⅔ CUP (38 G) CANDIED ORANGE FLOWERS; ALTERNATIVE: CANDIED
ORANGE PEEL

1. Follow the instructions in the recipe for closed *katayef* until step 3.

2. Spread fresh *ashta* in the middle of each pancake on the remaining third of the pancakes. Fold them a little bit, so that the filling is still visible.

3. Garnish with ground pistachios and candied orange flowers. Serve the sugar syrup on the side (see recipe on page 136).

Fresh Ashta

LEBANESE CLOTTED CREAM

⅖ CUP

Since it is difficult to come by ashta, you can make your own. But it requires time and patience.

2½ CUPS (593 ML) WHIPPING CREAM

1. Pour the cream into a heatproof bowl and allow to simmer gently in a water bath for 1½ to 3 hours, until it begins to thicken. Do not stir the cream and make sure that it does not boil.

2. Remove the bowl and let it stand in the refrigerator for at least 12 hours. Lift up the thick and creamy surface with a perforated ladle. Stir until it is smooth and supple.

القطايف المفتوحة

غير مغلقة

٨ حصص صغيرة

آخر ثلث من فطاير القطايف تقدم غير مغلقة أي أن الحشوة ظاهرة. تُستعمل القشطة الطازجة في لبنان، نوع من الكريم الكثيف Clotted cream. وهنا يمكننا الإستعاضة عنه بكريم فريش أو ريكوتّا ricotta.

١/٣ ثلث العجنة الأساسية للقطايف، أنظر صفحة
٧ ديسيليتر قشطة طازجة، أنظر الوصفة أدناه،
جبنة الكيسو كاملة Keso، كريم فريش أو ريكوتّا ricotta.
١ ديسيليتر فستق حلبي مطحون
١ ديسيليتر زهور البرتقال المُحلاة، وكل مربى قشر البرتقال

١- أتبع الخطوات الموجودة في وصفة القطايف المغلقة الى نقطة ٣.

٢- ضع القشطة الطازجة في الثلث المتبقي من فطاير القطايف. أطويهم قليلاً حتى تبقى الحشوة ظاهرة.

٣- زيّنها بالفستق الحلبي المطحون وزهور البرتقال المحلاة. يقدّم القطر بجانب فطاير القطيفة.

القشطة الطازجة

قشطة الكريمة اللبنانية

لصعوبة الحصول قشطة طازجة يستطيع المرء أن يقوم بإعداد القشطة الخاصة به. ولكن ذلك يحتاج الو وقت وصبر.

٦ ديسيليتر كريمة الحليب Visp grädde

١- ضع الكريمة في إناء يتحمل الحرارة العالية ودعه يغلي بهدوء في حوض من الماء الساخن من ساعة ونصف الى ثلاث ساعات حتى تصبح كثيفة. لاتحرّك المحتويات وأحرص على عدم وصولها الى درجة الغليان.

٢- أرفع الإناء وضعه في الثلاجة لمدة ١٢ ساعة. أغرف السطح المتكثف بواسطة مغرفة مثقّبة. حرّك بشكل متوازن ومرن.

Ashta Pudding

6-8 PORTIONS

Ashta can also be made into a type of pudding that you can cook yourself.

6 CUPS (1⅓ L) MILK
2 CUPS (240 G) POWDERED SUGAR
⅖ CUP (51 G) CORNSTARCH
2 TABLESPOONS ROSE WATER
1 TABLESPOON ORANGE BLOSSOM WATER
OPTIONAL: RAISINS

1. Boil 5 cups (1⅛ liters) of milk, add powdered sugar, and whisk until the sugar has dissolved.

2. Dissolve the cornstarch in the remaining cold milk.

3. Let the pot stand over medium heat and add the thickener while whisking continuously.

4. When the milk begins to thicken, add the rose water and the orange blossom water.

5. Add raisins if you want. Garnish with candied orange flowers and ground pistachios.

القشطة المطبوخة

عدد الحصص: ٢ كيلو تقريبًا

حليب ٦ أكواب
نشاء ١/٢ كوب
سكر ناعم ٢ كوب
ماء زهر ١ ملعقة كبيرة
ماء الورد ٢ ملعقة كبيرة

١- نضع خمس أكواب من الحليب في طنجرة على النار، ونرفع الحرارة إلى درجة الغليان ثم نضيف السكر ونخفق بالشريط حتى يذوب السكر.

٢- نخفق في هذا الوقت، وعلى حدة، النشاء في كوب الحليب الباقي البارد.

٣- نضيف النشاء المذاب بالحليب إلى الحليب على النار ونحرّك بملعقة خشب على نار متوسطة الحرارة. وتحت تأثير الحرارة سيشتدّ النشاء، ويصبح أكثر لزوجة.

٤- نضيف عندها ماء الورد وماء الزهر ونخفق مجدداً لتوزيعهما جيداً في القشطة.

٥- كما يجب أن نخفق جيداً خلال صنع القشطة لئلا تظهر فيما بعد حبيبات النشاء غير الذائبة فيها.

٦- وهناك مَن يضيف الزبيب إلى القشطة، أما أنا فلا أحبّذ ذلك لأن الضيف قد يعتقد أن الزبيب قطع محروقة من القشطة. لذا أتركها بيضاء مثل الثلج لتجنّب أي سوء ظن.

Umm Ali

EGYPTIAN BREAD PUDDING

10 SERVINGS

*This is an ancient dessert that is served "to the poor and rich alike,"
both in Egypt and at the hotel buffets around the Arab world. It is
reminiscent of the Lebanese dish, aish el saraya, which is also made with
day-old bread.*

1⅓ POUNDS (600 G) DAY-OLD WHITE BREAD

4¼ CUPS (1 L) MILK

1 CUP (200 G) SUGAR

2 CUPS (473 ML) SWEETENED CONDENSED MILK

⅘ CUP (120 G) GOLDEN RAISINS

⅘ CUP (120 G) WALNUTS

1 TABLESPOON CINNAMON

1¾ CUPS (250 G) BLANCHED ALMONDS

⅘ CUP (98 G) PISTACHIO NUTS

1. Preheat the oven to 400°F (200°C). Cut off the crust from
   the bread. Pour milk over the bread and let it stand until the
   bread has softened.

2. Allow the bread to drain and place it in a saucepan. Add
   sugar and stir over medium heat until it turns into a smooth
   and doughy mixture.

3. Add the condensed milk, raisins, walnuts, and cinnamon.
   Coarsely chop the almonds and pistachios and add them.

4. Mix all ingredients together and pour into an ovenproof dish.

5. Put the dish in the oven for a few minutes until the surface
   has a nice golden–brown tone. Remove the dish, garnish with
   soaked raisins, and serve.

Tip!

*Once I met a French chef in Kuwait, who told me that he replaced the
day–old bread with day–old croissants, and he claimed that the result was
even better.*

الأم علي

خبز بايت ٦٠٠ غرام

حليب سائل ليتر

حليب مكثف محلى كوبان

زبيب كوب

جوز حبّ كوب

قرفة ناعمة ملعقة كبيرة

لوز مسلوق ومقشر كوبان

سكر كوب

فستق مسلوق ومقشر كوب

١- من وصفة شعبية بسيطة تقدمت وصفة الأم علي حتى أصحبت تقدم في بوفيهات أهم
الفنادق المصرية وحتى فنادق الدول العربية الكافة. وأشبهها نوعًا ما لوصفة عيش
السرايا اللبنانية. فالمبدأ نفسه: من خبز بايت، ولعدم رميه، تحضير وصفة حلويات!

٢- نرفع القشرة عن لبّ الخبز الإفرنجي ونغمره بالحليب السائل حتى تطرى.

٣- نصقيه من دون عصره ونضعه في وعاء على النار متوسطة ونقلبه مع السكر حتى
يبدأ يتحول إلى عجينة طرية.

٤- يضاف إليه الحليب المكثف المحلّى والزبيب والجوز والقرفة.

٥- تقلب المواد مع بعضها البعض ثم تسكب في جاط سيدخل الفرن ويزين سطحها
باللوز المسلوق والمقشر.

٦- يترك الجاط بضعة دقائق حتى يتلون سطحه ثم نخرجه ويوزع عليه الفستق ويقدم.

Baklava

SWEET ARABIC PASTRIES

25 PIECES

Baklava is a flaky pastry made out of layers of wafer-thin dough. They come in many different shapes and with all kinds of fillings. If you don't feel like making the dough, you can buy frozen phyllo dough, which works fine as a replacement.

3 CUPS (375 G) FLOUR
4 TABLESPOONS VEGETABLE OIL
A PINCH OF SALT
⅖ CUP (95 ML) LUKEWARM WATER
2 CUPS (256 G) CORNSTARCH

FILLING

2 CUPS (250 G) FINELY CHOPPED HAZELNUTS
1 CUP (200 G) SUGAR
OPTIONAL: ORANGE BLOSSOM WATER AND ROSE WATER
4 CUPS (900 G) BUTTER
2 CUPS (473 ML) SUGAR SYRUP (SEE RECIPE PAGE 136)
⅖–⅘ CUP (49–98 G) FINELY CHOPPED PISTACHIOS

1. Knead flour, oil, salt, and water for 15 minutes, until the dough becomes soft and smooth.

2. Cut the dough into 10 equal pieces.

3. Flour the work surface with cornstarch. Roll out the pieces to large circles, about 10 inches (25 cm) in diameter. The dough should be very thin, almost translucent.

4. Mix the chopped nuts with sugar and possibly some orange blossom water and rose water.

5. Stack 10 layers of dough on top of each other. Cut into small squares of 2 x 2 inches (5 x 5 cm).

6. Place a tablespoon of the nut filling in the middle of each square.

7. Fold the edges without sealing the corners. Melt the butter.

8. Place the pastries in a greased roasting pan and pour the melted butter over them.

9. Bake in the oven at 350°F (175°C) for about 30 minutes, or until they are golden brown.

10. Remove the tray from the oven and pour out the butter.

11. Pour warm sugar syrup over the pastries, and sprinkle with very finely chopped pistachios in the middle of each *baklava*. Allow to cool.

البقلاوة

عدد الحصص: ٣٠ حبّة تقريبًا

طحين ٣ كوب
زيت نباتي ٤ ملعقة كبيرة
ملح رشة بسيطة
ماء فاتر ١/٢ كوب
كاجو مجروش ٢ كوب
سمنة مذابة ٤ كوب
نشاء ٢ كوب
سكر ناعم ١ كوب

١- نخفق الطحين والزيت والملح والماء حتى نحصل على عجينة متماسكة وطريّة، ويتطلّب ذلك حوالي ربع ساعة.

٢- نقسم بعد ذلك العجينة إلى عشرة أقسام، نجعلها كريات صغيرة.

٣- نرش القليل من النشاء على الطاولة ونبدأ برّق الكريات الواحدة تلوَ الأخرى بشكل دوائر ذات قطر ٢٠ سنتم، ويجب أن تكون الدوائر رقيقة جداً وشفافة ويمكن أن يصل القطر إلى ٣٥ سنتم.

٤- أصبح الآن العجين جاهزا، وتتوقف الحشوة بداخله على الصنف الذي نريد صنعه.

Awamat

FRIED BALLS IN SUGAR SYRUP

12 PIECES

A traditional and very common treat in Lebanon. Crispy and sweet at the same time.

2½ CUPS (312 G) FLOUR
½ TEASPOON DRY YEAST
2½ CUPS (ABOUT 600 G) PLAIN YOGURT, SUCH AS GREEK YOGURT
5 CUPS (1⅕ L) VEGETABLE OIL
5 CUPS (1⅕ L) SUGAR SYRUP (SEE RECIPE ON PAGE 136)

1. Mix flour and dry yeast. Heat the yogurt to 125°F (50°C), add it, and work into a smooth batter.

2. Cover with a kitchen towel and allow to rise for 1 hour in a warm place.

3. Heat the frying oil in a fryer or saucepan with a thick bottom. Pipe small balls directly into the oil with a pastry bag, or roll them by hand, and then lower them into the oil with a slotted spoon.

4. Deep-fry in batches until they are golden brown. Lift them up and drain on paper towels.

5. Soak them in sugar syrup for a few minutes and then place them on a serving platter or in a bowl.

العوامات

عدد الحصص: ١٢ حبّة أو كرة وسط تقريبًا

طحين ٢ ١/٢ كوب
لبن ٢ ١/٢ كوب
خميرة ١/٢ ملعقة صغيرة
قطر ٥ أكواب
زيت للقلي ٥ أكواب

١- نخلط الطحين مع الخميرة ونضيف إليه اللبن ونعجن حتى نحصل على عجينة متماسكة وسائلة.

٢- نضع غطاء على الوعاء ونتركها في مكان معتدل الحرارة حتى تختمر ويكبر حجمها ويستغرق ذلك حوالي ساعة ونصف.

٣- نضع المزيج بعد ذلك، أو قسماً منه، في كيس سكب ذي رأس حديدي مستدير، ونبدأ بتوزيع كريات صغيرة في الزيت الحامي ونقلبها فيه حتى تتلوّن جيدا، كما نستطيع التقاط العجينة باليد والضغط عليها بين الأصابع واليد فتخرج بين السبابة والإبهام فنلتقطها بملعقة صغيرة ونوزّع هذه الكريات بالزيت الحامي.

٤- نخرجها بعد ذلك من الزيت ونصفّيها جيداً ثم نغمسها في القطر ونضعها في جاط التقديم.

٥- نستطيع صنع العوامات أيضاً بالبطاطا المسلوقة التي تضاف إلى الطحين وتعجن معه بالماء (مقدار ٢ كوب من البطاطا المسلوقة والمطحونة على ٢ كوب من الطحين و ٢٫٥ من الماء).

Barazek

SESAME COOKIES

30–40 COOKIES

Sesame seeds are very popular in Arabic pastries and cookies. Here, we have dipped the cookies in a generous amount of sesame seeds.

1⅓ CUPS (156 G) SEMOLINA OR DURUM WHEAT FLOUR
6⅗ CUPS (800 G) FLOUR
1 CUP (200 G) SUGAR
⅔ CUP (51 G) DRY MILK POWDER
½ TABLESPOON DRY FRESH YEAST FOR SWEET DOUGHS
½ TABLESPOON MAHLAB (OPTIONAL)
1⅓ CUPS (300 G) BUTTER
1 CUP (237 ML) WATER
1⅓ CUPS (187 G) SESAME SEEDS
1 TABLESPOON MELTED BUTTER
1 TABLESPOON SUGAR SYRUP (SEE PAGE 136)
⅗ CUP (74 G) CHOPPED PISTACHIOS (NATURAL)

1. Preheat the oven to 450°F (230°C).

2. Mix semolina flour, flour, sugar, dry milk, yeast, and mahlab (if you are using it) in a bowl. Work the butter into the flour mix with your fingertips so that you get a crumbly dough, or mix briefly in a food processor.

3. Heat water to 125°F (50°C). Make a hollow in the center of the dough and pour the water into it, or add water into the food processor if you are using it. Work into a dough. It will be pretty sticky.

4. Roll the dough into small balls with lightly floured hands. Flatten them with your palms. Mix sesame seeds, melted butter, and sugar syrup. Press one side of the cake in the chopped pistachios. Press the other side in the sesame seeds mixture.

5. Place the cookies on a parchment paper–covered tray, and bake in the oven for about 10 minutes. Allow to cool and serve.

البرازق

عدد الحصص: ٢٠ حبّة صغيرة تقريبًا

طحين أبيض وسمسم ١ كيلو من كل صنف
طحين فرخة ١ كوب
سمنة ٣ أكواب
سكر وماء ٢ كوب من كل صنف
حليب بودرة ٣/٤ الكوب
خميرة ومحلب ١ ملعقة كبيرة من كل صنف
دبس الخروب (أو القطر) ٢ ملعقة كبيرة
زبدة سائلة ٢ ملعقة كبيرة
فستق حلبي مجروش ١ كوب

١– نخلط في وعاء الطحين الأبيض وطحين الفرخة والسمنة والسكر والحليب البودرة والخميرة والمحلب، ثم نصنع في وسطهما حفرة ونضع فيها الماء ونخلط الجميع حتى نحصل على عجينة متماسكة.

٢– نقطع هذه العجينة إلى كريات صغيرة ثم نكبسها برؤوس أصابعنا ونغلّف جهة بالسمسم الذي مزجناه مع الدبس والزبدة والجهة الثانية بالفستق المجروش.

٣– نصف الحبات في صينية ستدخل إلى فرن متوسط الحرارة لمدّة عشر دقائق ثم تقدّم باردة.

Mamool

FILLED SEMOLINA COOKIES

ABOUT 20 COOKIES

Traditionally, special wooden dishes are used for these cookies, one kind for each filling. Use what cookie dishes you may have.

DOUGH

6 CUPS (720 G) COARSELY GROUND SEMOLINA

1 CUP (120 G) FINELY GROUND SEMOLINA OR DURUM WHEAT
    FLOUR

3 CUPS (680 G) BUTTER

1 CUP (237 ML) ROSE WATER AND ORANGE BLOSSOM WATER, MIXED
    ACCORDING TO PREFERENCE

FILLING

2 CUPS (250 G) CHOPPED OR GROUND WALNUTS

2 CUPS (250 G) CHOPPED OR GROUND PISTACHIOS

2 CUPS (ABOUT 300 G) DATE PASTE OR MIXED DATES

2½ CUPS (500 G) GRANULATED SUGAR

3 TABLESPOONS ROSE WATER

½ TABLESPOON ORANGE BLOSSOM WATER

⅕ CUP (25 G) FLOUR

⅖ CUP (48 G) POWDERED SUGAR

1. Mix the two semolina varieties in a bowl.

2. Add the melted butter and work together by hand.

3. Mix the rose water with the orange blossom water according to your preferred proportions. Knead until you have a smooth and soft dough.

4. Allow the dough to rest for at least 1 hour. The longer you let it sit, the more flavor it will have.

5. Make three different kinds of filling by adding ⅘ cups of granulated sugar to the walnuts, to the pistachios, and to the date paste. Dash with a little bit of rose water and orange blossom water over all three fillings.

6. Shape small balls out of about 2 tablespoons of the dough. Flatten them between your palms and add a tablespoon of filling in the center of each. Pinch at the edges.

7. Sprinkle little cookie molds with flour and place the ball inside, carefully pressing to cover the entire mold.

8. Empty the molds by beating the backs lightly with a spoon. Place them on parchment paper on a baking sheet and bake at 450°F (225°C) for 30 minutes, or until they get some color.

9. Allow to cool. Sprinkle the nut–filled variations with a lot of powdered sugar and leave the ones with the date filling as they are.

المعمول

عدد الحصص: ٢٠ حبّة صغيرة تقريبًا

١٢ حبّة كبيرة تقريبًا

العجينة

سميد ٦ أكواب

طحين فرخة ١ كوب

زبدة أو سمنة سائلة ٣ أكواب

ماء زهر وماء ورد ١ كوب (النسب حسب الرغبة)

الحشوات

جوز مجروش ٢ كوب

فستق مجروش ٢ كوب

تمر ٢ كوب

سكر ناعم ٣ كوب

ماء الورد ٣ ملاعق كبيرة

ماء الزهر ١/٢ ملعقة كبيرة

سكر بودرة ٣ أكواب

١- نخلط السميد مع طحين الفرخة ونضعه في وعاء عميق.

٢- نضيف إليه الزبدة أو السمنة السائلة ونفركهما حتى نحصل على فرك متماسك، والبعض يضيف السكر والحليب والخميرة، في هذه المرحلة.

٣- نضيف إلى الخليط ماء الورد وماء الزهر ونمزج المواد بعضها ببعض حتى نحصل على عجينة متماسكة وطريّة.

٤- نضع العجين على طاولة العمل ونتركها مدّة ساعة، مع العلم أنّ هناك من يتركها فترة أطول بكثير وذلك لتتداخل المواد بعضها ببعض أكثر وتتبادل النكهات فيما بينها.

٥- نهيئ الحشوات وذلك بوضع كوب من السكر مع كل صنف ونوزّع ماء الورد وماء الزهر على الحشوات الثلاث.

٦- نستعمل لصنع المعمول قوالب خشبية بحيث يكون لكل صنف من الحشوة قالب خشبيّ خاص به، وذلك كي نستطيع تمييز الحشوات بعضها من بعض.

٧- يكون قالب التمر إجمالاً مستديراً أو مفلطحا. أما قالب الجوز فيتخذ شكلاً هرمياً مستدير الجوانب، بينما يتّخذ قالب الفستق شكلاً بيضويًّا مستطيلا.

٨- وهناك قوالب كبيرة للحبات الكبيرة وقوالب صغيرة للحبات الصغيرة.

٩- نصنع كريات صغيرة بمقدار ملعقة صغيرة لكل كرة نضعها في وسط كفّ اليد اليسرى ونضغط عليها قليلاً بكف اليد اليمنى ونضع فيها الحشوة ونعطيها شكل الكرة الثانية.

١٠- نضع الحبة في القالب المطابق لها ونضغط قليلا. يجب أن تملأ الكرة القالب جيداً وإذا التصقت فيه نرش بداخله القليل من التطبيع قبل البدء بالتطبيع القليل من طحين الفرخة.

١١- نصفّ حبات المعمول في صينية ونحرص على عدم وضع الحبات الكبيرة مع الحبات الصغيرة بل نفصلها وندخل الصينية الفرن (الصغيرة ٢٠٠ درجة مئوية. الكبيرة ٢١٠ درجة مئوية حتى تتلوّن الحبات وتنضج العجينة).

١٢- نترك الحبات تبرد ثم نرشها بالسكر البودرة (عدا التمر) وتصبح جاهزة للتقديم.

Ma'karoons

FRIED CONES IN SUGAR SYRUP

ABOUT 30 PIECES

A really sweet treat, both inside and on the outside. These are very different compared to the European variation of macaroons.

4 CUPS (500 G) FLOUR
1 CUP (120 G) SEMOLINA OR DURUM WHEAT FLOUR
1 TABLESPOON DRY YEAST
6⅓ CUPS (1½ L) FRYING OIL
2 TABLESPOONS SUGAR
4 TABLESPOONS ANISE
1 TABLESPOON MAHLAB (OPTIONAL)
1 CUP (237 ML) WATER
4 CUPS (946 ML) SUGAR SYRUP, SEE THE RECIPE BELOW

1. Mix flour, semolina or durum wheat flour, and dry yeast.

   Add 1½ cups (355 ml) of oil and mix well.

2. Add sugar, anise, *mahlab*, and hot water (125°F/50°C). Knead to a smooth and firm dough. Allow to rise for 1 hour in a warm place.

3. Divide the dough into about 30 small rectangular pieces.

4. Press the dough pieces against the coarse surface of a dome–shaped grater so that they bend. The dough gets a pattern from the grater. My grandmother used to use a wicker basket to create a pattern.

5. Heat the remaining oil and fry the cookies. Turn them occasionally until they are golden brown. Allow them to drain and soak them in sugar syrup for a few minutes.

6. Serve as soon as they have cooled.

LEBANESE SUGAR SYRUP

¾–1¼ CUPS (200–300 ML)

This Lebanese sugar syrup is quite thick and flavored with rose water and orange blossom water. Everyone loves this syrup, and it is used in many desserts.

1 CUP (200 G) SUGAR
1 CUP (237 ML) WATER
1 TEASPOON LEMON JUICE
1 TEASPOON ROSE WATER
1 TEASPOON ORANGE BLOSSOM WATER

1. Dissolve the sugar in water in a saucepan over medium heat without stirring.

2. Bring to a boil, and scoop away the white foam that forms on the surface.

3. Simmer for about 20 minutes, then add the lemon juice. Lemon juice preserves the color and prevents the syrup from solidifying.

4. Add the rose water and the orange blossom water. Simmer for a few more minutes. Allow to cool.

المعكرون

طحين وقطر ٤ أكواب من كل صنف
طحين فرخة وماء ١ كوب من كل صنف
زيت للقلي ٦ أكواب
سكر ٢ ملعقة كبيرة
يانسون ٤ ملاعق كبيرة
محلب ناعم ١ ملعقة صغيرة
خميرة ١ ملعقة كبيرة

١- يخلط الطحين العادي مع طحين الفرخة والخميرة ويضاف إليه كوباً ونصف من الزيت ويخلطان معاً حتى نحصل على الفرك

٢- نضيف إليه السكر واليانسون والمحلب ثم الماء. نعجن المواد حتى نحصل على عجينة متماسكة وشديدة ونتركها ترتاح لفترة ساعة

٣- نقسمها بعد ذلك إلى كريات صغيرة ثم نعطيها شكل الأصابع

٤- على الجهة الخشنة من المبشرة، نضع قطعة العجين ونضغط عليها نحو الأسفل بحيث يلفّ بعضها على بعض، وتحمل على جهتها الخارجية آثار ثقوب المبشرة وكانت جدتي تستعمل صينية مصنوعة من قش للفّ حبات المعكرون عليها.

٥- نضع الحبات فيما تبقّى من الزيت وقد حمّيناه على النار ونقلبها فيه حتى تتلوّن جيدا. نصفّيها ونضعها في القطر ونكبسها فيه لبضع دقائق

٦- تقدّم فوراً أو عندما تبرد

القَطر اللبناني

القَطر اللبناني كثيف الى حدّ ما ويُضاف اليه مذاقات مختلفة مثل ماء الورد وماء الزهر ويستعمل في عدد كبير من الحلويات والجميع يحبونه.

٢ ١/٢ ديسليتر سكَر
٢ ١/٢ ديسليتر ماء
١ ملعقة شاي من عصير الليمون الحامض
١ ملعقة شاي ماء الورد
١ ملعقة شاي ماء الزهر

١- يُذاب السكَر في الماء في قدر (طنجرة) على حرارة متوسطة بدون تحريكه.

٢- دعي المزيج يغلي وإجمعي الرغوة المتكونة على السطح بواسطة ملعقة وإرميها خارجاً.

٣- دعي المزيج يغلي لمدة ٢٠ دقيقة وبعد ذلك أضيفي اليه عصير الليمون الحامض. وهذا يحافظ على لون مزيج القطر ويمنعه من التصلب.

٤- أضيفي ماء الورد وماء الزهر ودعيه يغلي لبضع دقائق. وبعدها أطفئي النار تحته. دعيه يبرد قليلاً وبعد ذلك يصبح جاهزاً للإستعمال.

Nammoura

SOFT SEMOLINA CAKE

ABOUT 20 PIECES

Everyone loves this classic Lebanese cake, especially the little ones.

2 TEASPOONS BAKING POWDER
2 CUPS (450 G) BUTTER
4¾ CUPS COARSELY GROUND SEMOLINA
1 CUP (120 G) FINELY GROUND SEMOLINA OR DURUM WHEAT FLOUR
2 CUPS (400 G) SUGAR
2½ CUPS (593 ML) WATER OR PLAIN YOGURT, SUCH AS GREEK YOGURT
2 TEASPOONS TAHINI
1 CUP (140 G) BLANCHED AND PEELED WHOLE ALMONDS
3 CUPS (710 ML) SUGAR SYRUP (SEE RECIPE ON PAGE 136)

1. Mix baking powder, melted butter, and both semolina varieties.

2. If you are using water: dissolve the sugar in the water, pour it into the semolina mix, and stir well. If you are using yogurt: pour it directly into the semolina mixture, add sugar, and mix well.

3. Grease a round baking mold, about 12 inches (30 cm) in diameter, with tahini.

   Pour the batter in and garnish the cake with the almonds.

4. Bake at 400°F (200°C) for 30 to 45 minutes. Remove the cake from the oven and soak it with syrup.

5. Once it has cooled, cut it into squares and serve.

Tip!

You can also add coconut to the batter.

النمّورة

عدد الحصص: ٢٠ قطعة مربّعة وسط

سميد ٥ أكواب
طحين فرخة ١ كوب
لوز مسلوق ومقشر ١ كوب
زبدة أة سمنة ٢ كوب
سكر ناعم ٢ كوب
ماء أو لبن ٢ ١/٢ كوب
بيكنغ باودر ٢ ملعقة صغيرة
طحينة ٢ ملعقة كبيرة
قطر ٣ أكواب

١- نخلط السميد، طحين الفرخة والبيكنغ باودر والزبدة السائلة.

٢- إذا كنا نستعمل الماء نذوّب فيه السكر ونضيفه إلى الفرك ونخلطهما معاً حتى نحصل على عجينة متماسكة وطرية. أما إذا كنا نستعمل اللبن فنضيفه إلى الفرك مع السكر مباشرة.

٣- ندهن قعر وجوانب صينية مستديرة قطرها ٣٥ سنتم تقريباً، بالطحينة، ونسكب فيها العجينة الطريّة التي نزّين سطحها باللوز المسلوق والمقشر.

٤- ندخل الصينية فرناً شديد الحرارة (٢١٠ درجة مئوية) ونتركها فيه لمدّة نصف ساعة تقريباً أو ٤٥ دقيقة، وعند إخراجها من الفرن نرشها بالقطر.

٥- تقطع بعد ذلك إلى مكعبات وتقدّم.

ملاحظة:

نستطيع إضافة جوز الهند إلى مكوناتها.

Stoof

SOFT CAKE WITH TURMERIC AND ANISE

ABOUT 20 PIECES

This cake is not as sweet as Arabic pastries tend to be. It is known for its beautiful yellow color.

2½ CUPS (312 G) FLOUR

4 CUPS (480 G) FINELY GROUND SEMOLINA OR DURUM WHEAT FLOUR

1 TEASPOON BAKING POWDER

1 TABLESPOON TURMERIC

1 TABLESPOON ANISE SEEDS

1½ CUPS (350 G) BUTTER

3 CUPS (600 G) SUGAR

3 CUPS (710 ML) MILK

2 TABLESPOONS TAHINI

⅖ CUP (54 G) PINE NUTS OR SESAME SEEDS

1. Mix flour with semolina, baking powder, turmeric, and anise seeds.

2. Distribute the butter into the mixture and combine it with your fingers until it becomes a crumbly mass.

3. Dissolve the sugar in the milk and pour it into the flour mixture. Work it into a smooth batter.

4. Grease a round baking pan, about 12 inches (30 cm) in diameter, with tahini.

5. Pour the batter into the pan and decorate the surface with pine nuts or sesame seeds. Bake at 400°F (200°C) for about 30 minutes.

   Insert a thin wooden stick to check if the cake is ready. When the stick comes out dry, the cake is done.

6. Remove the cake from the oven and allow it to cool. Cut into squares and serve.

الصفوف

عدد الحصص: ٢٠ حبّة مربّعة

طحينة ٢ ملعقة كبيرة

طحين فرخة ٤ أكواب

طحين ٢ ١/٢ كوب

سكر ناعم ٣ أكواب

زبدة ١ ١/٢ كوب

حليب سائل ٣ أكواب

بيكنغ باودر ١ ملعقة صغيرة

عقدة صفراء ١ ملعقة كبيرة

يانسون ناعم ١ ملعقة كبيرة

صنوبر ١/٢ كوب

١- نخلط الطحين مع الفرخة والبيكنغ باودر والعقدة الصفراء واليانسون الناعم .

٢- نضيف إليه الزبدة ونفرك المزيج حتى نحصل على الفرك .

٣- نذوّب السكر في الحليب ونضيفه إلى الطحين ونخلط كل هذه المواد بعضها مع بعض حتى نحصل على عجينة متماسكة وطرية.

٤- ندهن قعر وجوانب صينية مستديرة قطرها ٣٠ سنتم تقريباً بالطحينة.

٥- نسكب العجينة في الصينية ونجعل سطحها متوازياً ونورّع عليه الصنوبر أو السمسم، ثم ندخل الصينية إلى فرن شديد الحرارة (٢٠٠ درجة مئوية) لمّدة نصف ساعة تقريباً ونعرف أنها نضجت وذلك بإدخال سكين رفيع في وسطها وإذا خرج وليس عليه أي أثر للعجين فهذا يعني أن الوصفة أصبحت جاهزة .

٦- نخرجها بعد ذلك ونتركها تبرد ثم نقطعها إلى مكعبات.

Fig Marmalade with Grape Molasses

2–3 JARS

I want to share this recipe with you because it contains grape molasses, which is such an important element in our cuisine. It consists of grapes that have been boiled to form a syrup. This way all the minerals are concentrated, and it is a healthier and tastier alternative to sugar. You can replace it with sugar, but the taste will not be quite the same.

3 CUPS (450 G) DRIED FIGS
6 CUPS (ABOUT 1 KG) GRAPE MOLASSES (OR 5 CUPS GRANULATED SUGAR)
2 CUPS (288 G) SESAME SEEDS

1. Cut the figs into small cubes.

2. Boil the grape molasses and add the figs.

3. Simmer over low heat, while slowly stirring. Add the sesame seeds once the figs have softened.

4. Allow to cool. Pour into clean and hot glass jars.

5. Serve with desserts, on a piece of toast, or with a good cheese.

مربى التين
مع دبس العنب

عدد الحصص: ١٠-١٢ وجبة

قصدت أن أذكر لكم هذه الوصفة، لتروا كم كان استعمال دبس العنب منتشراً ومهماً. ففي وصفة مربى التين، نستعمل اليوم السكر للتحلية، أما فيما مضى فكانوا يستعملون الدبس. وتجدر الإشارة إلى أن نكهة الدبس مع التين تضفي على الوصفة طعماً لذيذاً ونكهة مميزة لا تتوفّر للتين مع السكر الذي يتحوّل بدوره إلى قطر فقط.

دبس العنب ٦ أكوابَ
تين مجفّف ١/٢ كيلو
سمسم ٢ كوب

١– تلاحظون في الصورة تحت الفخارة المحتوية على المربى، التين المشرّح، والذي يشمّس حتى يجف ويجمد.

٢– فبعد عملية التجفيف، نقطعه إلى قطع صغيرة.

٣– نضع الدبس على النار حتى يغلي، ثم نضيف إليه قطع التين.

٤– نباشر بالتحريك على مهل، على نار هادئة، وقبل الوصول إلى النضوج الكامل أي قبل إطفاء النار بقليل، نضيف السمسم ونتابع التحريك.

٥– عند النضوج الكامل، نطفئ النار ونترك المربى حتى يبرد، ثم نوزعه في أنية لحفظه.

Candied Orange Peel

20 PIECES

Orange flavor is very popular and is used in many Arabic sweets. Candied orange peels are used in many desserts, but you can also eat them as they are.

5 ORANGES
WATER
SUGAR

1. Wash the oranges, grate the peels lightly, and cut them into four wedges. Remove the pulp.

2. Place the orange zest in a saucepan, cover with water, and simmer until the peels are tender. Rinse with cold water.

3. Allow the peels to soak in the sugar syrup for 3 to 4 days. Change the water every day.

4. Dry and roll up the peels lengthwise. If you want to, you can tie a piece of string around each peel to prevent it from unfolding.

5. Weigh the orange peels and measure the same amount of sugar. Cover the bottom of a heavy-based saucepan with some of the sugar. Place an orange peel on top, and continue alternating sugar and peels. Gently cook over low heat until the peels are soft and the syrup has thickened.

6. Take the orange peels out of the saucepan and allow them to cool, then roll them in sugar and serve with desserts, such as the *ashta* pudding on page 123. Candied orange flowers look beautiful with any dessert.

مربى
قشور البرتقال

عدد الحصص: ٢٠ حبّة تقريبًا

١- تغسل حبات الأبو صفير ثم تبرش قليلا، وتقطع كل حبة إلى أربعة حصوص، وينزع عنها اللبّ.

٢- يسلق القشر، وعند نضوجه، يرفع ويوضع في وعاء جديد يغمره الماء البارد.

٣- ينقع لثلاثة أيام مع تغيير الماء كل يوم، وهنالك مَن يجعلها أربعة. والهدف من ذلك إزالة المرورة المعروفة للأبو صفير.

٤- بعد مرور ذلك الوقت، يصفّى القشر، ونلف كلّ حبة على بعضها (وهنالك مَن يستعين بخيط لإبقائها على شكلها الملفوف).

٥- نزن السكر بما يعادل وزن القشر، ونوزّع في كعب وعاء طبقة من السكر، نضيف إليها طبقة من القشر الملفوف، ثم السكر، ثم القشر، وهكذا دواليك حتى يمتلئ الوعاء، فنضعه على نار خفيفة.

٦- نرفع القشر، وعندما يبرد، نغلّفه بالسكر.

Taktiaa

DATE–FILLED SESAME COOKIES

ABOUT 35 COOKIES

Dates are a common feature in our sweets. Their creamy sweetness is perfect for fillings in cookies and other treats.

8 cups (1 kg) flour
about 1 cup (250 g) butter
1.8 ounces (50 g) mahlab, alternative: a little bit of grated bitter almonds
a pinch of grated nutmeg
⅕ cup (47 ml) milk
⅗ cup (120 g) sugar
1.8 ounces (50 g) yeast
1½ cups (355 ml) water
a pinch of vanilla sugar
⅖ cup (95 ml) rose water
⅖ cup (95 ml) orange blossom water
⅗ cup (142 ml) carob molasses, alternative: syrup or molasses
7 cups (1 kg) sesame seeds
18 ounces (500 g) date paste or mixed and dried dates
⅘ cup (100 g) pistachios

1. Preheat the oven to 450°F (225°C). Put the flour in a bowl. Add the melted butter.
2. Mix *mahlab* (or a little bit of bitter almonds) with nutmeg, milk, and sugar. Add the flour and butter. Stir until the butter absorbs the spices.
3. Dissolve the yeast in lukewarm water and then mix with the other ingredients. Work into a smooth dough. Allow it to rest for 10 minutes.
4. Mix vanilla sugar, rose water, orange blossom water, and carob molasses (or syrup or molasses) with sesame seeds and work together thoroughly so that the seeds absorb the flavors.
5. Remove the pits from the dates and blend or mash them if you are not using date paste. Roll into small balls. Roll slightly larger balls out of the dough, press a finger into the middle to make a hole. Fill the dough ball with the date ball and seal the hole. Roll the balls in the sesame seeds mixture and sprinkle with chopped pistachios.
6. Bake the cookies for 15 minutes until they have a nice color on all sides.

التقطيعة

المكونات:
طحين كيلو
سمنة ٢٥٠ غرام
محلب ٥٠ غرام
حليب ٥٠ غرام
برش جوزة الطيب رشة
خميرة ٥٠ غرام
ماء ٣٥٠ غرام
سمسم للزينة
دبس الخروب ١٥٠ غرام
فانيليا رشة
ماء زهر ١٠٠ غرام
ماء ورد ١٠٠ غرام
تمر مطحون ٥٠٠ غرام
فستق حلبي، مسلوق ومقشر (للزينة) ١٠٠ غرام

١– نضع الطحين، ثم تفتر الزبدة ونضيفها فوق الطحين.

٢– نضيف المحلب مع برش جوزة الطيب، بعدها نفرك الخليط مع بعضه البعض حتى تشرب مكونات السمنة.

٣– نذوب الخميرة في الماء ونضيفها إلى المزيج، ثم نعجن المكونات حتى الإندماج ونترك العجينة لمدة ١٠ دقائق كي ترتاح.

٤– نضع رشة الفانيليا مع ماء الزهر وماء الورد فوق السمسم وبعد ذلك نضيف الدبس ونفرك الكلّ مع بعضه البعض حتى تمتص حبة السمسم المكونات.

٥– تقسم العجينة إلى قسمين:

القسم الأول نستعمله بشكل حبال ومن ثم نقطعها بطول ٥ سنتم،
والقسم الثاني نجوف قسمًا من العجينة ونضع في قلبها حشوة التمر ونلتها بالسمسم، ثم نزيّن حبة التقطيعة بحبة الفستف المسلوق والمقشر.

٦– تخبز التقطيعة على درجة حرارة ٢٢٠ درجة كعب، و ٢٢٠ درجة وجه لمدة ١٥ دقيقة.

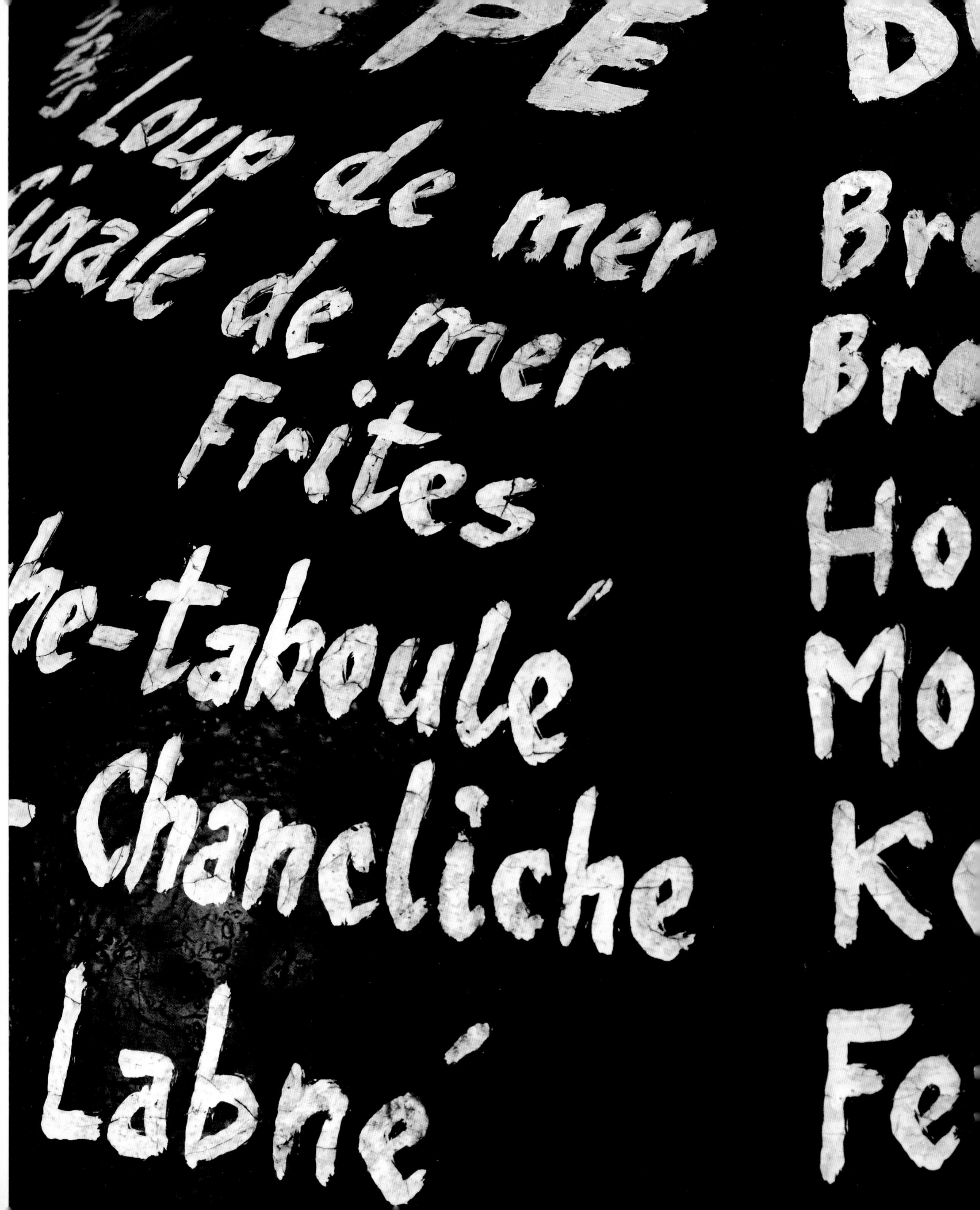

loup de mer

de mer

de mer

Frites

he-taboulé

Chancliche

Labné

Quick Reference Guide to Lebanese Cuisine

ASHTA
Used in desserts and available in two variations. Fresh ashta is similar to British clotted cream. You can make it yourself, but it is time consuming. Can be replaced with ricotta, crème fraiche, or sour cream.
Ashta pudding is cooked, and it is similar to rice pudding.

BULGUR
Whole wheat grains that have been steamed, dried, and crushed. Available in different sizes. A staple in the entire Middle East, it is included in many Lebanese dishes.

CAROB MOLASSES
Syrup made from carob, or St. John's bread, as the fruit is also called. Aromatic sweetener used in baking or with yogurt. Can be found in Middle Eastern shops.

DRIED LIME, LOOMI
Distinct flavor that does not have much in common with our regular lime. Available to buy whole or as a powder. Look for it in Middle Eastern shops.

FREEKEH
Roasted green wheat with a nutty and delicious flavor. Used about the same way as rice. Available in assorted oriental stores. Can be replaced with wheat berries or brown rice.

GHEE
Clarified butter that is extremely durable and heat-resistant, and therefore common in hot Arab countries, but also in India. Available to buy in a jar in Middle Eastern shops and well-stocked supermarkets. Can be replaced with oil or regular butter.

GRAPE MOLASSES, PEKMEZ
It consists of grape juice that has been boiled down to a sweet syrup. Used as a more aromatic and healthy replacement for sugar, and it is a popular feature in Lebanon's culinary inheritance. You can find it in Middle Eastern shops.

KIBBEH
Collective name for ground meat dishes. The word means "ball," but kibbeh comes in all shapes and forms, including flat pies. It consists mostly of bulgur and ground meat or fish, and can have all kinds of fillings.

LABNEH
Lebanese yogurt that is thick and creamy. Can be replaced with plain yogurt, such as Greek or Turkish yogurt.

LIBA BREAD
Large, flat, round bread, similar to pita bread but without the pocket. Common in various dishes or on the side of main courses. Can be found at Middle Eastern bakeries and well-stocked grocery stores. Can be replaced with other types of flat breads or pita bread.

MAHLAB

A spice with strong flavor, reminiscent of bitter almonds. It is made from the kernels of Mahaleb cherries, and it is used in small amounts in cooking. Can be found in Middle Eastern shops.

MASTIC

A type of liquid resin from the mastic bush, used in cooking in some parts of the world. Can be difficult to find in the United States, but look for it in Middle Eastern shops or Greek stores.

ORANGE BLOSSOM WATER

Popular condiment with an aromatic scent. Used primarily for sweets but also in coffee. Produced from bitter orange flowers, not orange flowers. Sold at Middle Eastern shops and well-stocked supermarkets.

POMEGRANATE SYRUP

Tart condiment consisting of very concentrated pomegranate juice. Can be found at Middle Eastern shops. Can be replaced with balsamic cream.

PURSLANE

An ancient cultivated plant with mildly acidic leaves. Easy to grow. Mainly used in the popular salad *fatoush*.

QAWARMA

Meat confit (meat that has been cooked slowly in its own fat) was very common in the olden days, but can still be found in many parts of Lebanon.

ROSE WATER

Aromatic flavor with the scent of rose. Very common in sweets and desserts. Can be found in Middle Eastern shops, well-stocked grocery stores, and some pharmacies.

SAVORY

Herb that is common in fatoush, a very popular salad.

SUMAC

Red spice made from the dried berries of the sumac tree. It has a very tart flavor and can be replaced with lemon. Can be found in Middle Eastern shops and well-stocked supermarkets.

TAHINI

Sesame paste made from ground sesame seeds. Has a very special flavor. Light sesame paste is often used in Lebanon, but there is also dark sesame paste. You can find tahini in Middle Eastern shops, health food stores, and well-stocked supermarkets.

TARATOR

Classic dressing made with sesame paste that is served with falafel, among other dishes.

ZAATAR

Spice blend containing oregano and other spices.

PE

...s loup de mer
...igale de mer mer
Frites
...he-taboulé
...Chancliche
Labné

DU
Bro
Bro
Ho
Mo
Ke
Fe

Recipe Index

دليل الوصفات العربي

دليلك الى المطبخ اللبناني

ماء الزهر APELSINBLOMSVATTEN
من المواد الشائعة لأضافة النكهة وهو ذو لمحات عطرية. يُستعمل بشكل أساسي في إعداد الحلويات، وفي القهوة أيضاً. يستخلص في الحقيقة من زهور النارنج وليس زهور البرتقال. يُباع في متاجر الشرق الأوسط والمتاجر التي تبيع جميع أنواع البضائع.

القشطة ASHTA
تُستعمل في الحلويات وتوجد بنوعين. القشطة الطازجة تشبه الكريمة البريطانية المخثّرة. يمكن للمرء إعدادها بنفسه رغم أن ذلك يتطلب بعض الوقت. ويمكن الإستعاضة عنها بإستعمال ricotta أو crème fraiche. بودينغ القشطة مطبوخ ويذّكر ببودينغ الرز لدينا.

البرغل BULGUR
حبات القمح القاسي التي تُغلى بالبخار، وتجفف ثم تُكسّر. توجد بأحجام مختلفة. مادة أساسية في الشرق الأوسط وتدخل في وجبات طعام لبنانية كثيرة.

دبس العنب، بيكميز DRUVMELASS, PEKMEZ
يتكون من عصير العنب الذي يُغلى ليصبح سائلاً مركّزاً. يُستعمل كبديل ذي مذاق لذيذ ومفيد بدلاً من السكّر وهو جزء مهم من تراث المطبخ اللبناني. يُباع في متاجر الشرق الأوسط.

الفريكة FREEKEH
قمح أخضر محمّص ذو مذاق لذيذ يشبه مذاق اللوز. ويستعمل تقريباً كما الرز. يمكن شراؤه من المتاجر الشرقية ذات تشكيلة السلع الكبيرة. ويمكن الإستعاضة عنها بقمح الطعام أو الرز الخام.

السمن GHEE
زبدة مستخلصة طويلة العمر الى حد كبير وتحتمل الحرارة العالية ولذلك فهي شائعة في البلدان العربية، وفي الهند أيضاً. تُباع معلبة في متاجر الشرق الأوسط ومتاجر المواد الغذائية التي تبيع جميع أنواع البضائع. يمكن الإستعاضة عنها بالزيت أو الزبدة العادية.

شراب الرمان المركّز (رُب الرمان) GRANATÄPPELSIRAP
من مواد إضافة النكهة ويتكون من عصير الرمان المركّز جداً. يُباع في متاجر الشرق الأوسط. ويمكن الإستعاضة عنه بكريم البلسميكو.

دبس الخرّوب KAROBMELASS
شراب مركّز مصنوع من الخرّوب، او خبز يوحنا كما يدعى أيضاً. وهو مادة للتحلية ذات رائحة عطرية يُستعمل في إعداد المعجنات أو مع اللبن الرائب. يُباع في متاجر الشرق الأوسط.

الكبّة KIBBEH
أسم يُطلق على مجموعة من وجبات اللحم المفروم. الكلمة تعني في الأصل "كرة"، ولكن الكبة توجد بأشكال مختلفة منها الفطائر المسطحة. تتكون على الأغلب من البرغل واللحم أو السمك المفروم، ويمكن أن تُحشى بمختلف الحشوات.

الزعتر البري KYNDEL
عشب يُستعمل عادة في سلطة الفتوش الشهيرة.

اللبنة LABNEH
اللبن الرائب اللبناني الطبيعي الكثيف. يمكن الإستعاضة عنه باللبن الرائب (اليوغهورت) من النوع اليوناني أو التركي.

الخبز اللبناني LIBABRÖD

خبز رقيق مسطح دائري الشكل، يذكّر بخبز البيتا ولكن بدون فراغ يفصل بين طبقتيه. يستعمل عادة مع الطعام ولأكل الطعام. يوجد في مخابز الشرق الأوسط ومتاجر الأغذية ذات التشكيلة الكبيرة من البضائع. يمكن الإستعاضة عنه بأنواع من الخبز الرقيق أو خبز البيتا.

المحلب MAHLAB

من التوابل الحادّة المذاق يُذكّر باللوز المرّ ويُنتج من نوى الكرز البري، ويستعمل بكميات صغيرة جداً في طهي الطعام. يُباع في متاجر الشرق الأوسط.

المستكة MASTIX

نوع من الراتينج السائل من شجرة المستكي ويستعمل في طهي الطعام في بعض بقاع العالم. قد يكون من الصعب العثور عليه في السويد، ولكن قد تعثر عليه في متاجر الشرق الأوسط أو المتاجر اليونانية.

البقلة PORTLAK

نبات قديم يتحدر من ثقافات عريقة له أوراق ذات طعم حامض معتدل. يمكن للمرء زراعته بنفسه. يُستعمل بشكل أساسي في إعداد سلطة الفتوش الشهيرة.

القاورمة QAWARMA

لحم يطبخ بطيئاً مع السمن وكان في السابق يشكّل النوع الأساسي للحم، غير أنه مايزال موجوداً في بعض مناطق لبنان.

ماء الورد ROSENVATTEN

من مواد إضافة النكهة ذو رائحة عطرية وفي رائحته نوطات من عطر الورد البلدي (الجوري). شائع جداً في إعداد حلوى المعجنات والحلويات. يُباع في متاجر الشرق الأوسط ومتاجر المواد الغذائية ذات التشكيلة الواسعة من السلع وفي بعض الصيدليات.

السماق SUMAK

بهار أحمر اللون من توت شجرة السماق. له مذاق حامض جداً ويمكن الإستعاضة عنه بحامض الليمون. يُباع في متاجر الشرق الأوسط ومتاجر المواد الغذائية ذات التشكيلة الواسعة من السلع.

الطحينة TAHINI

عجينة السمسم المعصور ولها مذاق خاص جداً. وتُستعمل الطحينة الفاتحة اللون في الطعام اللبناني، ولكن هناك أيضاً طحينة ذات لون داكن. تُباع الطحينة في متاجر الشرق الأوسط، وبعض متاجر الطب البديل، وكذلك في متاجر المواد الغذائية ذات التشكيلة الواسعة من السلع.

الطراطور TARATOR

صلصة كلاسيكية تُعدّ من عجينة السمسم ويوضع أحياناً على الفلافل.

الليمون المجفف TORKAD LIME, LOOMI

مادة لأضافة النكهة ليس لها أية سمات مشتركة مع الليمون الموجود لدينا. يمكن شراؤه كحبات غير مطحونة أو على شكل مسحوق. أبحث عنه في متاجر الشرق الأوسط.

الزعتر ZAATAR

خليط من التوابل يتكون من توابل مختلفة منها البردكوش (الأوريغانو).

إنها مدينته التي تنتشر فيها أكشاك الحراسة وصراخ الأطفال. والتي يلوّح الناس فيها للطاهي الذي يظهر في التلفزيون ويتبادلون معه بعض الجمل القصيرة من خلال نافذة السيارة الجانبية. يدٌّ على المقود والأخرى للشعب، حب وحضور. فجأة نصبح خلف أحد باعة الخضروات الذي يجّر عربته القديمة المتهالكة أمامنا وتصبح حركة المرور بطيئة أكثر مما كانت. تشرق إبتسامة كبيرة أكثر من أي وقت مضى على محيا الشيف رمزي، فيستدير نحوي قائلاً:

« رؤية هؤلاءالرجال بعرباتهم القديمة يعيدني الى ذكريات طفولتي، ولكنه أيضاً نموذجي لشعورنا بالجودة العالية في الفواكه والخضروات. وهذا يمنح أملاً كبيراً بأن الإستمتاع بالطعام مازال له مستقبل رائع في عالم التكنلوجيا المتطورة!»

بو ماسّر Bo Masser

كتاب الطبخ العربي الجديد هذا الذي بين يديك أُعدّ في مدرسة Al Kafaât Catering School، التي تقع في أعالي سفح الجبل في المنصورية عند الطرف الشرقي من بيروت.

تجولنا على قمة الجبل، نحن بعض الضيوف السويديين ورمزي، بين أطلال بعض الحضارات العظيمة المندثرة، التي تجمعت منذ آلاف السنين طبقة بعد أخرى.هنا عمل الناس وكدّوا، وإرتفعوا في البنيان وعشقوا بلغات عديدة. ولايسع المرء سوى أن يشعر بالخشوع أمام تلك اللحظة وتلك البصمات التي أبدعها الإنسان على أرضنا هذه. وربما كان الغبار المتساقط من حذائي هو وحده الذي ترك آثاراً سريعة الزوال لأقدامي عندما عدتُ الى قاعات مدرسة الكفاءات.

في أسفل الوادي تنزهت على أطلال قنطرة من العهد الروماني. فعلى النهر في قاع الوادي بنى الرومان قنطرة قطعوا أحجارها من الجبال الكلسية والحجر الرملي، وأصبح من الممكن إيصال المياه الى بيروت بمساعدة تلك القناة. محاطاً بجميع هذه الآثار التاريخية يقود رمزي مدرسة تعليم الطبخ للمطاعم لشباب هذا اليوم ويحاضر لتأكيد أهمية حسن الضيافة والمعرفة المتعلقة بطهي الطعام الراقي ذي الجودة العالية. الإحترام والتواضع. جذور عميقة لانهاية لها، في تربة حملت الكثير من الأفكار والأحلام خلال آلاف السنين. عندما كنا في المدرسة كان رمزي يساعدنا بينما ترتسم على وجهه إبتسامة الرضا، وكان يبدو راضياً تماماً، بينما كنا نكتشف أسرار المطبخ العربي.

يؤكد رمزي أن العرب يحبّون المطبخ اللبناني، وبشكل عام فالمطبخ العربي محدود جداً بحكم المناخ والجغرافيا. فأكثر البلدان العربية تتكوّن من شريط ساحلي طويل ومناطق ضيقة صالحة للزراعة إضافة الى مناطق صحراوية شاسعة في الجزء الداخلي، مما يؤثر على إنتاج المواد الغذائية. وهكذا يصبح إختيار المواد التي يمكن زراعتها محدود جداً أيضاً بحكم طبيعة المنطقة. ويختلف لبنان في هذا المجال بأن لديه أربعة فصول واضحة المعالم ومنفصلة عن بعضها بالإضافة الى وفرة المياه في هذا البلد. ويشكّل هذان العاملان فروقاً كبيرة جداً مقارنة بالبلدان العربية الأخرى. لهذا السبب يملك المطبخ اللبناني إمكانيات كبيرة لتنويع وجباته الغذائية. ويحبّ جميع العرب ذلك، فهم يشعرون بالمذاق ويشعرون بالقرب منه والإنتماء اليه.

كانت اللحوم على الدوام شكلاً من الترف في المطبخ العربي، أما اليوم فهناك مزارع كبيرة لتربية الأبقار والأغنام. وفي اليمن كانت منذ مئات السنين سوق مشهورة جداً للتوابل، حيث ترسو السفن القادمة من الهند فتصل بضائعها الى منطقة الخليج سالكة هذا الطريق. ثُم تُنقل البضائع من الخليج الى لبنان وبعد ذلك الى أوربا. حول هذا السوق التاريخي للتوابل وطريق القوافل التي تنقلها نشأت وجبات غذائية عديدة بمذاقات حادّة إنطلاقاً من جميع التوابل والبهارات وكانت تقدم سوية مع بضاعة أخرى غالية القيمة هي الأرز البزمتي. الذي كان يُقدم بشكل رئيسي مع وجبات السمك. الطعام في منطقة الخليج يمتاز بالقوة، ولكنه ليس متنوعاً، وتشكّل الفواكه الجافة والزبدة العمود الفقري فيه.

المملكة العربية السعودية لديها «الكبسة» المكوّنة من اللحم والسمن — المستخرج من حليب البقر أو الغنم، وهي وجبة طُوّرت لمقاومة حرارة المناخ الصحراوي. ومع هذه الإمكانات المحدودة يجد المرء عدداً قليلاً فقط من أصناف الطعام المتخصص في عموم العالم العربي. وربما لهذا السبب لايوجد الى جانب لبنان سوى عدد قليل من البلدان التي لديها تقاليد غنية ومجموعة واسعة ومتنوعة من أطباق الطعام. فالمغرب وتونس والجزائر وليبيا لديها جميعاً ثقافة طعام غنية جداً. ويستطيع المرء الإستماع هناك بوجبات كثيرة رائعة، خصوصاً وجبات الأسماك، واللحوم والدواجن، إضافة الى الحلويات.

يقول رمزي: نحن محظوظون إذ نعيش نعمة المناخ الأكثر اعتدالاً، وقبل كل شئ ليس لدينا مناطق صحراوية. فأنواع الفواكه والخضروات أكثر من أن تُعدّ في لبنان. ولدينا المنطقة الساحلية وسهل البقاع الأخضر، كما لدينا وفرة في المياه ومناخ أكثر إعتدالاً. وهنالك اليوم منتجون عديدون للحوم مثل لحوم الدجاج والضأن والغنم. وهناك أيضاً بعض منتجات لحم الخنزير.

يُغطي الثلج جميع القرى الجبلية في فصل الشتاء فتتقطع السبل والطرقات بالناس، أو هكذا كانت على الأقل. وتصبح العوائل سجينة في منازلها، مما خلق تطوّراً ملحوظاً في ثقافة تحضير الطعام في الصيف والخريف. ولم يكن ذلك يشمل فقط الفواكه كالمشمش والعنب والتين بل أيضاً الخضروات كالكوسة (القرع الإفرنجي) والباذنجان والطماطم التي كان يتم تجفيفها على سطوح المنازل. كان البرغل من المنتجات المهمة للتخزين في فصل الشتاء وهو نوع خاص من القمح المكّسر يُستعمل في صناعة الكبة والتبولة. ويختلف البرغل عن ذلك النوع الذي يمكن إقتناؤه في أوربا بكونه أكثر خشونة، فهو على الأكثر كالحبة الكاملة.

في السابق كان يتم حفظ اللحوم بأساليب عديدة لعدم وجود الثلاجات والمجمّدات. فكان اللحم يُطحن ويُغلى بالدهن، ليوضع بعد ذلك في عُلب تُغطى بطبقة عريضة من الدهون. بهذه الطريقة يصبح اللحم صالحاً للإستعمال لمدة ستة أشهر. أما الآن فقد أصبح من الصعب شراء اللحم المحفوظ بهذه الطريقة. كان العمل اليومي مجهداً خلال فصل الشتاء والناس يحتاجون الى طعام قوي ودسم.

أصبح لبنان الدولة الأولى في المنطقة في مجال الفنادق الكبيرة الفخمة بسبب موقعه المتميز. وصار اللبنانيون روّاداً في عالم السياحة وساهموا في تطوير فن تذوّق الطعام وتقاليد الحرفة والمعارف المتعلقة بها. والطلب كبير جداً اليوم من جميع الفنادق على الطهاة اللبنانيين.

توصّل الطهاة اللبنانيون الى استعمال العنب بطرق عديدة ومختلفة. فخلال القرن التاسع عشر عندما كان السكّر سلعة شحيحة في القرى النائية أرادوا مع ذلك إعداد بعض الحلويات. فإستعملوا حينها عصير العنب بغليه على نار هادئة حتى يصبح كثيفاً ويحصل على حلاوة مركّزة. وكان شراب العنب المركّز (دبس العنب) هذا يُستخدم مثلاً في تحضير الكعك والبسكويت. أما الليمون فهو شجرة تنمو قريباً من المناطق الساحلية، ولاتنبت على الجبال إطلاقاً. وعندما كان الطهاة يحتاجون الى الليمون الحامض كانوا يحلّون هذه المشكلة بإستعمال العنب. فقد كانوا يأخذون عصير العنب غير الناضج، الذي يحتوي على كمية كبيرة من الحامض ويستخدمونه في السلطات والتبولة. المذاق الحلو والحامض من ذات العنصر!

حافظ المطبخ اللبناني على العديد من عناصره التقليدية بواسطة إستعمال مختلف أنواع الخضروات، والبقوليات، والحبوب وزيت الزيتون. وهو طعام صحي في نواحي كثيرة. إذ إن البصل الطري والثوم هما من العناصر التي لها تأثير مفيد على ضغط الدم.

يؤكد الشيف رمزي قائلاً: لقد عانينا من العزلة في بعض الفترات خلال العقود الأخيرة. عشنا داخل حدود بلدنا منفصلين ومقطوعين عمّا يحصل في الخارج. ولكن بين 1992–1994 إفتُتحت فجأة في لبنان مطاعم ماكدونالدز وستاربوكس والعديد من مطاعم تقديم الطعام السريع التي تنضوي تحت سلسلة مطاعم عالمية. وشعر الناس بأن ذلك كان إنفتاحاً واسعاً على العالم. هرع الناس الى تلك المطاعم ليحصلوا من تلك الأشياء الجديدة على إحساس يدغدغ مشاعرهم. ولكنهم عادوا سريعاً الى الطعام الذي يحبونه أكثر من أي شئ آخر. ومازالت المطاعم اللبنانية هي الرقم الأصعب في المنطقة وتجتذب العديد من الناس أكثر من أي مطبخ آخر.

في السنوات الأخيرة برزت ظاهرة جديدة. هي المقهى اللبناني. وحازت هذه النزعة على شعبية واسعة، خصوصاً بين الشباب. وتقدّم المقاهي اللبنانية مقبّلات لبنانية الى جانب القهوة إضافة الى الأركيلة (الشيشة). والأركيلة موضة عصرية لدى الشباب، ولكنها ليست على الإطلاق تقليد لبناني. أما في الفنادق فتُقدم في قوائم الطعام مزيجاً من الوجبات اللبنانية والأوربية.

يصحبني رمزي في جولة بسيارته في حركة المرور التي تزخر بالفوضى وفي نفس الوقت بإبداء الكثير من الإحترام للآخرين. ويشرح لي ذلك مشيراً الى حركة المرور المرنة رغم الكثافة الخانقة فيها: لقد عشنا دون قانون ولانظام لعقود طويلة فتعلمنا كيف يحترم أحدنا الآخر.

في المرة الأخيرة حين عاد الشيف رمزي الى ليون لإكمال دراسته في الجامعة كان يحمل معه فكرة أن يتعلم أسرار ثقافة المخابز الفرنسية. فذهب لهذا السبب ليتعلم لدى خبير الحلويات Bernard Moine، رئيس Syndicat des Pâtissiers-Boulangers (إتحاد خبازي الحلويات). ونال رمزي في نهاية المطاف عضوية الشرف في الإتحاد.

أصبح رمزي جاهزاً للسفر الى لبنان. في عام 1993 أعاد تنظيم وتحديث مدرسة تعليم الطبخ للمطاعم انطلاقاً من معلوماته التي إكتسبها في أوربا. كان البرنامج الدراسي قديماً ولكنه إستطاع الإستفادة من مهاراته في فن المخابز الفرنسية ودراساته الأوربية الأخرى.

في عام ١٩٩٤ إتصل تلفزيون المستقبل بالشيف رمزي. كان تلفزيون المستقبل قد بدأ للتوّ بث برامجه وكان مملوكاً لرئيس الوزراء اللبناني آنذاك رفيق الحريري. كان يتمّ تصوير البرنامج وبثّه في السنتين الأولى في لبنان فقط. فأصبح رمزي في عداد المشاهير خلال فترة قصيرة. قرر تلفزيون المستقبل عام 1996 أن يبدأ البث عن طريق الأقمار الإصطناعية. في البرنامج الأول أعدّ رمزي وجبة طعام لبنانية وأجاب في نفس الوقت على مكالمات هاتفية من دبي، ولبنان، ومصر والعراق وأجزاء أخرى من العالم حيث كان المشاهدون يستطيعون رؤية البث الفضائي، وفي غرفة السيطرة في الأستوديو إستعانوا بطاقم عمل إضافي ليستطيعوا الإجابة على جميع المكالمات الهاتفية. بعد إنقضاء نصف ساعة تسلل المخرج الى إستوديو البث بهدوء ولوّح بيديه وهامساً: إستمر، إستمر! إستغرق البرنامج الإفتتاحي فترة ساعة وربع. أما اليوم فإن البرنامج شبه اليومي يستغرق ساعة كاملة.

قرّر تلفزيون المستقبل اصدار كتاب من تأليف الشيف رمزي يحتوي على وجبات طعام عالمية للسوق العربية. حقق الكتاب مبيعات تجاوزت 600 000 نسخة حتى اليوم، إذ صدرت طبعته الثالثة. ويقوم الشيف رمزي الآن بنفسه بنشر وتوزيع الكتاب. هناك الآن برنامج لدراسة الغرافيك في مدرسة الكفاءات التقنية وتمّ الإستثمار في شراء مطابع من هايدبيرغ. ويطبع التلاميذ الآن من هذا الكتاب ما يصل عدده الى خمسة آلاف نسخة كل ثلاثة أشهر. ويُستثمر الربح المتأتي من طباعة الكتاب في المدرسة نفسها.

ان النجاح الذي حققه الكتاب ساعد الشيف رمزي في تحقيق حلم ظل يساوره لفترة طويلة: إصدار كتاب عن الطعام اللبناني والموروث الثقافي اللبناني. فقام خلال سنتين بالتجوال في لبنان وزار جميع المدن القديمة وكل القرى الصغيرة النائية في بلده الحبيب. (يبلغ طول لبنان حوالي 200 كيلومتراً أما العرض فهو 50 كيلومتراً ويعيش فيه 4.2 مليون مواطن.)

بيع من الكتاب الثاني عن فن الطبخ اللبناني والعربي 20 000 نسخة في يومين فقط. وحقق الكتاب مبيعات تجاوزت 150 000 نسخة حتى اليوم. كانت الترجمة الأولى للكتاب الى اللغة الفرنسية. وحصل الإصدار الفرنسي في Gourmand World Cookbook Awards 2003 في برشلونة على جائزة أحسن كتاب للطبخ العربي في العالم Best Arabic Cookbook in the World.

في نفس العام، 2003، أُصيب ستوديو الشيف رمزي في تلفزيون المستقبل في بيروت بقنبلتين. في اليوم التالي قرر أن يبثّ برنامج الطهي بثاً حياً كالعادة، واقفاً في الأستوديو بين الركام والأنقاض، على الرغم من أن إحدى القنبلتين لم تكن قد إنفجرت. المكالمات التي إنهمرت عليه من جمهوره البالغ عشرة ملايين مشاهد حول العالم عبّرت عن تعاطفها وتشجيعها وأدانت جميع الأعمال الإرهابية. بعد ذلك توقفّ بث البرنامج لمدة أربعة أشهر لإعادة بناء الأستوديو.

الطبّاخ ذو الإبتسامة المشرقة

كل من رأى الشيف رمزي في القنوات الفضائية التلفزيونية يعرف أنه يبتسم دائماً بلطف حميم، ولم نكن نحن استثناءً فقد منحنا إبتسامة رائعة عندما أتينا لنقوم بإعداد كتاب الطبخ هذا. يبدو ضخماً في النظرة الأولى والإنطباع الأول، بالطبع ولكن إشعاع الكاريزما الذي يملكه يطغي على ما سواه. تشعر عند الإقتراب منه أنه خجول على نحو ما ويُبدي، بتواضع جمّ، إهتماماً كبيراً ليجد الفريق السويدي طريقه دون عناء. وهو حذر عندما يصل الأمر لأنْ يتحدثّ عن نفسه أو يُظهر ذاته الخاصة. لم يكن طريقه الى عدة الطبخ والتعليم الشعبي الذي يديره اليوم يسيراً على الإطلاق. مع ذلك، فكل إستدارة، وكل قياس وكل خطوة تبدو منطقية للغاية عند النظر في مرأة الماضي. عندما يُدعى رمزي للحديث عن معنى الطعام، واللقاءات، والثقافة والشعور بالذات — يبدأ بالتغريد، يحتدم بالغليان ويخفض صوته بشكل مدروس، فالطعام شئ جديّ، الطعام هو السعادة. تعال معنا لتلقي بالطاهي المبتسم على الدوام رمزي من بيروت.

وُلد رمزي شويري عام 1970 في بيروت من عائلة تضم أربعة أطفال، أختان وأخ إضافة اليه. دمرت حرب 1976 أجزاءً كثيرة من بيروت وأتت كذلك على منزل عائلة رمزي. بقيّ الأب نديم في بيروت بينما إنتقل أفراد العائلة الآخرون الى ليون في فرنسا. حيث يوجد مقر راهبات *La Congrégation Notre Dame des Apôtres*. وقد ساعدت الراهبات نديم منذ البداية بشكل فاعل عندما أسس مؤسسة الكفاءات في عام 1957 وأحتفظوا معه بصداقة تمتدّ الى فترة طويلة.

أسس نديم مدرسة لتعليم فن الطبخ في المطاعم كجزء من مؤسسة كفاءات، لمساعدة ذوي الإحتياجات الخاصة والشباب الذين يعانون من صعوبات إقتصادية.

بقيت الأم ليلى والأطفال عاماً واحداً في فرنسا وعادوا بعد أن إنتهت الحرب في 1977. إستيقظ حب الطبخ في وقت مبكر لدى رمزي. وعندما عاد الى لبنان وهو في عمر السادسة كان يساعد أمه في تحريك الطعام في القدور والطناجر، حتى إنه يستطيع الآن أن يتذكر الروائح العطرية المختلفة للطعام.

إضطرت ليلى للهرب الى أوربا ثلاث مرات أخرى مع الأطفال. خلال هذه الفترة إستطاع رمزي إكمال دراسة الفلسفة وحصل على علامات جيدة في الإقتصاد والحقوق فتمكن من الدخول الى جامعة ليون 2.

قرر الإبن والأب شويري (السيد شويري الأب يفضل أن يتهجّى أسمه بالإنجليزية) أن يبذل شويري الشاب (رمزي يفضل أن يتهجّى أسمه بالفرنسية) قصارى جهده ويقوم بأفضل مايستطيع في تلك الظروف التي كان يمرّ بها كلاجئ. قام رمزي في فصل الصيف بتقديم طلب للإلتحاق بفرع جامعة لندن في بورن ماوث لدراسة فن الطبخ.

مرة أخرى يعود رمزي الى ليون ويستمر في دراسته الإخرى في مجالي الإقتصاد والحقوق. كانت المحاضرات في أوقات ما بعد الظهر والمساء. وكان رمزي متحمساً للعودة الى بيروت ليتمكن من دعم المؤسسة. ووجد أخيراً فرصة سانحة لتعلّم المزيد من العمل التطبيقي في مجال المطاعم. لذلك عمد طوال العام القادم الى النهوض منذ الساعة الرابعة والنصف صباحاً كل يوم ليبدأ عمله من الخامسة والربع الى الساعة الثانية عشرة ظهراً حيث كان يأخذ حافلة النقل العام ذاهباً الى الجامعة. وكان يتدرب على الوجه الخصوص لدى Jean Masson في مطعم *La Minaudière* المشهور عالمياً.

عراقة وانفتاح

من خلال موقعه الجغرافي منح العالم العربي ظروفاً خاصة جداً لسكانه لأنتاج المواد الغذائية. ذلك أن بيئاته الساحلية الممتدة لمسافات طويلة والمناطق الصحراوية في العمق هي المحيط الذي يستطيع فيه البشر زراعة موادهم الغذائية وإبداع ثقافتهم الخاصة بالطعام بشكل عام. وقد قامت هنا العديد من الحضارات المتطورة، وكان ممراً للعديد من الطرق التجارية المهمة، التي ساهمت في تكوين ثقافة الطعام العربيةً.

هذه المنطقة تشكّل جسراً يصل بين البحر المتوسط والشرق. وقد عبر وأستوطن بشر من مختلف أنحاء العالم في بلدي، لبنان، حيث يشكّل همزة وصل بين قارات عديدة. وبسبب ثرواته الطبيعية والماء الصالح للشرب عبر الناس من هنا أو حطوا رحالهم بشكل دائم. عاش الشعب اللبناني في حدود بلده مع عدد من الحضارات العملاقة: فالإغريقيين، والبيزنطيين، والروم، والفينيقيين، والأتراك والفرنسيين — تركوا جميعاً بعد رحيلهم آثاراً تدّل عليهم. وقد رحب الشعب اللبناني وأبدى احترامه لجميع المجموعات السياسية والدينية في بلده الأخضر.

تحت هذه المؤثرات العميقة تمّ الحفاظ على المطبخ اللبناني وأصبح ذا سمات تقليدية واضحة.
حاولتُ في التلفزيون أن أقوم بطهي وجبات تدمج بين ثقافات مختلفة وتتكون من الطعام اللبناني ووجبات أخرى ذات طابع عالمي. وجاءت ردود الفعل بشكل فوريّ، لم يحب الناس ذلك! إتصل المشاهدون بالإستوديو وأعلنوا عن شكواهم بأصوات عالية: "أطبخ سباغيتي أو لازانيا، ولكن لا تمزج ذلك مع الطعام اللبناني!" كان المشاهدون يرغبون بمعرفة جميع أسرار الطعام اللبناني الأصيل.

لكن جمهوري في التلفزيون يريد أيضاً أن يتعلم عن ثقافات الطعام الإخرى. فإذا عرف المرء تقاليده الخاصة وتاريخه يصبح من السهل عليه فهم وإحترام الثقافات الأخرى. وقد خرج الطعام العربي، واللبناني بشكل خاص، الى العالم بفضل جميع أولئك الذين يسافرون. فنحن نلتقي ونستمتع سوية بوجبة طعام شهية. قد يكون بإمكان الطعام أن يمدّ الجسور بين شعوب العالم ويقرّب بيننا حين نأكل مع بعضنا أو نقتسم ثقافات طعام الآخرين.

التقيت قبل سنوات بالناشرة أنجيلا هولم من السويد في حفل جائزة Gourmand World Cookbook Awards في بكين. إذ اجتمعنا سوية مع اشخاص أخرين من بقاع العالم المختلفة لنشارك الآخرين معارفنا وحبنا للطعام اللذيذ والراقي. وعندما أرادت أن تجلب معها طاقم العمل السويدي لتقوم بإعداد كتاب عن المأكولات العربية كان شرفاً لنا أن ندعوهم الى منطقة المنصورية ومدرسة الكفاءات لتعليم فنون الطهي Al Kafaât's Catering School. في الطرف الشرقي من بيروت.

علمني والدي الحبيب: "أنت تملك ماتعطي — ولاتملك ما لاتعطي." وها أنا أعطيك ميراثي في الطبخ.

الشيف رمزي

I WANT TO THANK ALL THE PEOPLE OF LEBANON FOR THEIR KIND HOSPITALITY.

أودّ أن أشكر الشعب اللبناني كلّه على كرم الضيافة

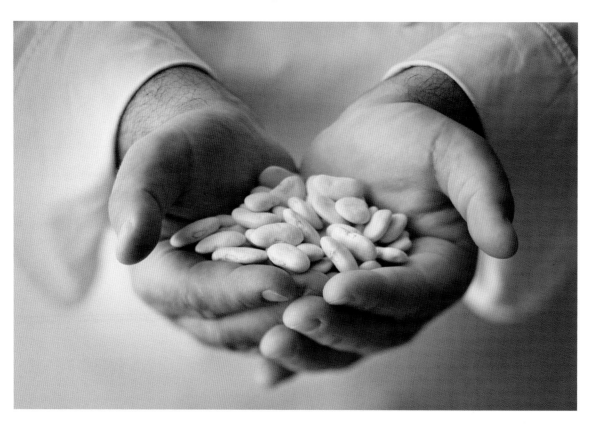

Chef Ramzi